THE PATTERN OF REDEMPTION

An In-Depth Study of God's Unconditional Love

GREGORY C. OLIVER

Cover and Interior Layout by 2025 Harvest Creek Publishing and Design, www.harvestcreek.net

Every effort was made to ensure that the information contained in this book, including online references, was accurate at the time of publication.

Ordering Information: Churches, associations, and others can receive discounts on quantity purchases. For details, please contact the author using the information listed at the back of the book.

The Pattern of Redemption—1st ed.

ISBN: 978-1-961641-40-2

Printed in the United States of America

PRAISE FOR THIS BOOK

Greg Oliver is a devoted student and passionate lover of God's Word. He invites the reader to journey with him as he plumbs the depths of both Old and New Testament Scripture, revealing the heart of God to redeem men and women to Himself through salvation in Jesus Christ. The themes and patterns Greg uncovers in familiar passages—scenes we may have read many times but never fully grasped—will draw you in and keep you turning the pages. This book will not only deepen your understanding of Scripture but also your love for the God who still speaks to us through it.

Sarah Stephens
Director of Ministries, Celebration Church, Woodlands, TX

Greg's writing style is captivating, engaging, and thought-provoking, making it difficult to put his book down. He makes it easy to connect the dots and uncover the types and shadows of God's plan for Redemption found throughout the Old and New Testaments, all the while emphasizing practical applications of this study to our own lives as believers. This book is a worthwhile investment of your time and attention.

Brian H. Bennett, MD, MPH
Global Occupational Health Director (retired), Huntsman Corporation

Greg Oliver has created an intriguing study of human Redemption. Whether you are new to studying the scriptures or someone who is very familiar with Biblical themes, this book will have a lasting effect. Greg is a lifelong student of God's word and a faithful follower of Jesus Christ. He creatively weaves in-depth thoughts of how God's love not only draws us to Him but also how God's saving grace leads us on a journey of faith and fulfillment. This book is an excellent study for individuals or groups. Readers will be blessed as they learn more about Redemption through some of the impactful events in the Bible.

Samuel Granberry, AAMS
Financial Advisor, Edward Jones

CONTENTS

FOREWORD

The Pattern of Redemption is a refreshing, in-depth study of sound biblical truth. Just as a child learns through consistent repetition and application, the reiteration of divine patterns throughout Scripture is given to benefit all humanity regarding God's most significant work: Salvation!

The Word says:

They serve in a system of worship that is only a copy,
a shadow of the real one in heaven.
For when Moses was getting ready to build the Tabernacle,
God gave him this warning:
"Be sure that you make everything according to the pattern
I have shown you here on the mountain."
HEBREWS 8:5 (NLT)

The history of automotive prototypes is a story of gradual development from rudimentary, hand-built models to sophisticated digital simulations. Early prototypes were often crafted from materials like wood, clay, and metal, requiring significant time and manual effort. Using scale models allowed for the visualization and refinement of designs before full-scale prototypes.

As such, most biblical scholars agree that Old Testament prototypes of people, events, or objects foreshadow New Testament realities—particularly the work of the Incarnate Word (John 1:1, 14 KJV). It should be noted that these types are not exact replicas, but imperfect representations that point toward a greater truth or fulfillment, which is Christ.

In the text, the author details a holistic view regarding the continuum of biblical patterns relative to salvation. Beginning with Creation, the Fall of Man, and through the formation of Israel with their covenant worship of the God of Abraham, Isaac, and Jacob, we see the *Pattern of*

Redemption repeated: Blood, Water, and Spirit. And these are fulfilled in Jesus Christ with His Death, Burial, and Resurrection.

From the new believer to the most senior disciple among us, I challenge you to glean from the hundreds of hours of research that a study like this demands. This book is not a frivolous, superficial review; rather, it is an in-depth study that will strengthen your faith and increase your knowledge of God.

Open your Bible and heart to God, asking him to reveal the meaning of Scripture to you just like he did for the disciples:

Then he opened their minds so they could understand the Scriptures.
LUKE 24:45 (NIV)

Charles Johnson, Pastor
Greater Life Church, New Braunfels, TX

INTRODUCTION

Patterns are common in many facets of our lives. It is not unusual to encounter patterns in nature, mathematics, architectural designs, music, etc. Humans tend to be drawn to patterns, especially those that are easily identifiable. Perhaps our keen observation of patterns was one reason God repeatedly choreographed His pattern of Redemption across the Bible.

To many Christians, the Old and New Testaments are so vastly different in tone that they appear to be complete opposites of one another. Even those who have spent a lifetime attending church and reading the Bible often see the Old Testament as an ancient history of the Israeli nation. Some are confused by the details of the Law and ceremonial rituals of the Tabernacle and are inclined to ignore the Old Testament entirely.

With precision and Biblical evidence, this book will show you the parallels between events in the Old Testament and the redemption pattern of the Gospel of Jesus Christ. These Bible studies will establish the repeating pattern of the Gospel, sometimes hidden within accounts in the Old Testament. Once you complete these studies, you should clearly understand the rigor with which God orchestrated history to accentuate His Son, Jesus Christ, and His plan for redeeming humanity.

I recommend that you examine these Bible studies in the order presented in this book. As you will learn, some of these studies build upon concepts explored in previous studies. Taking the studies out of order may add complexity to comprehending the principles presented.

Since I do not subscribe to any religious organization, these Bible studies do not align specifically with any Christian denomination. Instead, they were designed to lead the serious and open-minded Christian, or new believer, to Biblical truths. That being said, I recognize that certain Biblical ideas might clash with the beliefs of many Christian denominations. It is not my intention to offend anyone with these studies.

Regarding English translations of the Bible, while none are as accurate as the original texts, some are more exact than others. I recommend carefully considering which Bible translation is best for you as you explore these studies. With over 200 versions in over 70 languages, there are two distinct Bible reading approaches. *Word-for-Word* maintains the original language's words and structure while remaining clear. With the *Thought-for-Thought* approach, meaning in the original language is prioritized without sacrificing accuracy. Both methods hold significance, and several online apps feature multiple translations. To help you pick a suitable translation, see Figure 1 (below), sourced from the popular Bible app, *Biblegateway.com.*

My hope and prayer is that everyone who explores these Bible studies will be blessed by the Word and discover the truth of God's pattern for spiritual Redemption.

Gregory C. Oliver

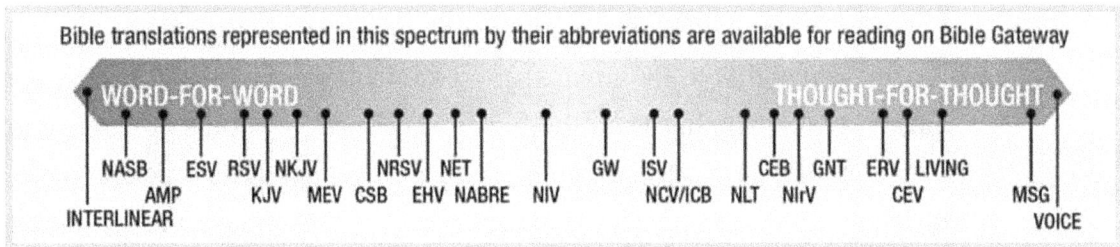

Bible translations represented in this spectrum by their abbreviations are available for reading on Bible Gateway

WORD-FOR-WORD   THOUGHT-FOR-THOUGHT

NASB | ESV RSV | NKJV | NRSV | NET | | GW | ISV | | CEB | GNT | ERV | LIVING | | MSG
AMP   KJV   MEV   CSB   EHV   NABRE   NIV   NCV/ICB   NLT   NIrV   CEV   VOICE
INTERLINEAR

Figure 1 - Bible Translation Guide

Scan this QR code to learn more about the Word-for-Word and Thought-for-Thought approaches to Bible reading.

STUDY ONE: *God's Creation*

OPENING PRAYER:

Heavenly Father, thank you for creating us in your image and breathing life into us. As we study your Word, we desire to understand better and become more like you. We open our minds and our hearts to receive your Word. Let understanding and fresh revelations come to each of us through this study. May your Word strengthen our faith and trust in you. We give you all the praise in the Holy Name of Jesus. Amen.

INTRODUCTION:

We will never forget the Christmas when we gifted our kids an enormous set of Legos. Watching how creative the kids became after receiving that gift was amazing. They assembled awesome works from their creative imaginations in just a few short days. I was so proud of their accomplishments (and still am).

However, the thought occurred to me that, in reality, they did not actually create anything at all. Consider this: Where did the material come from to mold the plastic that formed the Lego blocks? Where did the pigments come from that gave the blocks their unique colors?

Although mankind has become incredibly knowledgeable in manipulating, rearranging, and altering the material and elements around us, God alone can create something from nothing. God does not need a resume. But if He ever did, this would be an excellent skill to list!

Imagine, if you can, a dimension without time or space. A dimension where matter does not exist; only God exists, and He is infinite. As we contemplate the reality of God, many questions come to mind, such as:

- What about the angels? When did they first appear on the scene?
- Does God have a dwelling place?
- Why did God decide to create the universe?

The list of questions is endless. Unfortunately, our human limitations prohibit us from fully comprehending the full breadth of our God. There is much about Creation that we may never fully grasp.

However, the study of God's Creation is an incredible journey. Many books have been written specifically about this subject. Your goal in this study is not to become an authority on the subject, but to gain a basic understanding of the order of God's Creation. Understanding Creation will aid your deeper Bible study.

Regarding scientific theories versus the Bible, this study is predicated on the fact (or belief) that the Bible holds the truth. Therefore, such scientific theories and debates are not included in the scope of this study. If you wish to pursue theories and debates further, I refer you to Eric Metaxas's book *Is Atheism Dead?*

As you will learn in this study, the Bible declares that the universe was created in six days. However, in II Peter 3:8, we learn that 1000 "earth" days are as one day with God. Consider this as you contemplate the time frame of God's Creation.

God created the Universe in six days.

STUDY:

Read the following scripture passages and record your thoughts in the spaces provided.

DAY 1: GENESIS 1:1-5

What was created?

How was it created?

NOTE: Although light and darkness were created on Day 1, time did not begin until Day 4.

DAY 2: GENESIS 1:6-8

What was created?

How was it created?

DEFINITION: firmament (raqia in Hebrew)—an expanse.

DAY 3: GENESIS 1:9-13

What was created?

How was it created?

Notice the order of the day was: "...the evening and the morning."

DAY 4: GENESIS 1:14-19

What was created?

How was it created?

Note the beginning of time on Day 4.

DAY 5: GENESIS 1:20-23

What was created?

How was it created?

Scientific evidence confirms that life began in the sea.

DAY 6: GENESIS 1:24-31

What was created?

How was it created?

Numerology is common in the Bible:

6 = Number for man   7 = Number for God (completeness / perfection)

DAY 7: GENESIS 2:1-3

What was created?

What action did God take?

In the Jewish culture, including the Law of Moses, the seventh day of the week (the Sabbath) was holy and a time for rest. This pattern was predicated and patterned by the Creation when God rested on the seventh day after His act of Creation. The number "7" is significant throughout the Bible and implies completeness. Sometimes, this number also represents the fullness of God.

Now, let's turn our attention to John's writing regarding God's Creation. Fill in the blanks for these key passages:

JOHN 1:1 (KJV)

In the beginning was the _____, and the _____ was with God, and the _____ was God.

"Word" in the Greek text is *Logos*. The definition of Logos includes four attributes:

1. A collection of thoughts, which are
2. Related to speaking and thinking,

(cont'd next page)

3. Reasoning or motive, and

4. Divine reason or plan.

With this definition in mind, what is the meaning of John 1:1?

JOHN 1:3 (KJV)

All things were made by _____; and without _____ was not anything made that was made.

The Scripture below provides additional insight, referencing Christ Jesus:

> *Who is the image of the invisible God, the firstborn of every creature:*
> *For by Him were all things created, that are in heaven, and that are in Earth, visible*
> *and invisible, whether they be thrones, or dominions, or principalities, or powers:*
> *all things were created by Him and for Him:*
> *Colossians 1:15-16 (KJV)*

JOHN 1:10 (KJV)

He was in the _____, and the _____ was made by him, and the _____ knew him not.

Who is the Scripture referencing in this verse?

How can Jesus be both the Creator and a part of the world He created?

JOHN 1:14 (KJV)

And the _____ was made _____, and dwelt among us, (and we beheld his glory, the glory as of the only begotten of the _____,) full of grace and truth.

How was the Word made flesh?

CONCLUSION:

Before time began, there was only God and His thoughts. We can only imagine what it must have been like when the Thinker became the Creator and spoke the universe into existence. Scientists believe the universe began with a massive explosion of matter, which continues to expand.

If this were the case, I suggest that Genesis 1:3 describes such an event when God *said*, "Let there be light." And BANG—all matter and elements were formed, followed by an immense explosion. Even today, scientists have concluded that the universe is still expanding. I believe this will continue until God says, "Stop expanding." The King James translation of the Bible chose the word "firmament" to describe this concept. In Hebrew, this word is *raqia*, which means expansion.

Notice how time is depicted after each creative event. In keeping with this approach, the Jewish nation begins its day in the evening (6 p.m., or the 12th hour of the day, based on the sundial). Their day begins six hours ahead of the modern clock (see Appendix E). Understanding this difference is essential to your progress in these studies, especially when you study the Passover.

We read in Genesis 1:20-23 that sea life was created (day 5) before land life (day 6). This is consistent with scientific evidence; life began in the sea. Humans were created by God on day 6. Genesis 1:27 states that humankind was created in "God's own image."

Obviously, this does not refer to man's anatomy since the Bible then clarifies that He created both male and female. What, then, is the image of man? And further, what is the image of God? This topic will be explored more in a subsequent study.

The apostle John confirms in his writing (the book of John, Chapter 1) that the Word of God spoke the universe into existence. It is difficult to imagine that God (the Word) became flesh (human) and dwelt among humanity. It is almost beyond comprehension to know how God could create all things, then become human, essentially becoming part of what He had created. He created Himself in a human form. We will examine this further in a later study.

Bible scholars estimate there are around 300 Messianic prophecies in the Bible. The definition of *Messiah* (Hebrew) or *Christ* (Greek interpretation of Messiah) means "the anointed one." However, one historical definition states that the Messiah (i.e., Christ) is "the anointed flesh of God." As you study the Creation in Genesis and John, it becomes evident that Jesus was 100% God, while also being 100% human. Undeniably, Jesus, the Messiah/Christ, was involved in the Creation.

God rested on the seventh day. His creative work was complete.

SELF-REFLECTION:

What inferences have you drawn from this study?

What new information did you gain from these passages?

Describe the revelations you received from Study One and how they strengthened your belief in God.

STUDY TWO: *Image of Man*

OPENING PRAYER:

Heavenly Father, thank you for creating us with a spirit and a living soul. As we study your Word, open our understanding and reveal your truth to each of us. We prepare our minds and our hearts to receive your Word. Let the power of your Word transform each of us through this study. May your everlasting Word strengthen our faith and trust in you. We give you all the praise in the Holy Name of Jesus. Amen.

INTRODUCTION:

Amazingly, some people try to project a certain image. Let's be honest: We all know exactly what I am talking about! Years ago, I knew a man who wanted to convey the image of a rough, tough cowboy-type. He could *dress* the part and somewhat even *act* the part, but he didn't have a clue how to ride a horse or rope a calf.

I propose that there is a much broader perspective of the image of mankind than the type of persona someone wishes to project. In the previous study, you were presented with the study of God's Creation. The last act of God's Creation was the Creation of mankind. Recall that mankind was created on Day Six. In Biblical numerology, the number six, therefore, signifies man. You'll understand the importance of this numerology as you continue through the studies.

Of all the splendor of God's Creation, humans are the most unique and complex. What sets humans apart from the rest of Creation? As we strive to better understand God by exploring His Word, we must develop a firm comprehension of who we are. By doing so, we can then better understand God and His image.

In Study One, you read Genesis 1:27, which states, "God created man in His own image." The obvious question that follows is, "What is the image of man in the Bible and Creation?" As you will learn in Study Two, the image of man is much more than the physical attributes of a human, e.g., one head, two eyes, two ears, a nose, a mouth, two arms, two legs, etc.

In most English translations of the Bible, the word "image" comes from the Hebrew word *selem*, which means to shadow, a phantom or illusion, resemblance, or having the likeness of. When we consider how magnificent God is, it is humbling to realize that we were created in His likeness.

The study of man's image is important for two main reasons:

1. Once we understand the image of man, we will then understand the image of God.
2. As we consider the fall and Redemption of mankind, it is crucial to understand how they affect man's image.

Psalm 139:14 declares, "I am fearfully and wonderfully made."

STUDY:

Read the following scripture passages and record your thoughts in the spaces provided.

Genesis 1:26-27 and Genesis 2:7

From your readings: On what day was mankind created?

Humans were created in whose image?

When God breathed life into man, what did man become?

The Bible says in Genesis 1:27 that God created both male and female in His own image. Therefore, we can assume that the image of God is much more complicated than the physical appearance (i.e., beyond just the physical anatomy of a man).

Genesis 2:7 (KJV) states that God breathed the breath of life into the man that He created, and he became a "living soul." A living soul separates humans from God's other creations. From these scriptures, you can get a partial glimpse into the image of man; mankind has a body and a living soul. However, one additional aspect of the image of man will be presented in the last portion of this study. Before we cover this, let's review a few more key points regarding the creation of man:

Read: Genesis 2:8-25 and Genesis 3:20
What were the names of the first man and woman?

How did God create the first woman?

What two trees did God plant in the Garden of Eden? (see Genesis 2:9)

Name the four rivers that flowed from the Garden of Eden (described in Genesis 2:10-13):

Fill in the blanks for these key passages:

GENESIS 2:9 (KJV)

And out of the ground made the Lord God to grow every tree that is pleasant to the sight, and good for food; the tree of _____ also in the midst of the Garden, and the tree of the _____.

GENESIS 2:17 (KJV)

But of the tree of the knowledge of good and evil, thou shalt not eat of it: for in the _____ that thou eatest thereof thou shalt surely _____.

What was Adam's punishment if God learned that he had eaten from the tree of the knowledge of good and evil?

When would the punishment be imposed?

In the second chapter of Genesis, we are provided with deeper insight into God's Creation. Here we find the details regarding the habitat (the Garden of Eden) of the first man and woman (Adam and Eve). The Garden was a paradise for God's humanity. Varieties of trees and food were available to them there.

Adam and Eve were naked in the Garden, yet unaware of their nakedness. Although the scope of this book does not include a detailed study of the seven dimensions of time that span the Bible, the time Adam and Eve spent in the Garden of Eden has been coined the "Dispensation of Innocence" (See Appendix C).

Genesis 2:21-23 describes the account of the creation of Eve, the first woman. Adam was created first. Then, God caused Adam to fall into a deep sleep ("*tardema*" in Hebrew). While asleep, God created Eve from Adam's side. Most Bible translations reference the word "rib" as being removed from Adam to create Eve. That said, the Hebrew word *tsela* was translated as rib in this passage. However, this word has a much broader definition, which is: side, chamber, rib, beam, or plank. This same word is used to describe the sides of the Ark of the Covenant (see Exodus 25:12).

Although the first humans lived in God's paradise with almost unlimited freedom, God gave them one commandment. In Genesis 2:17 (KJV), God commands, "But of the tree of the knowledge of good and evil, thou shalt not eat of it: for in the day that thou eatest thereof thou shalt surely die." Adam and Eve were also given free will to obey or disobey God's commandment. However, God clearly stated that the punishment for disobedience was death; an immediate death would occur (the day you disobey, you will die).

Returning our attention to the image of man, the following reference includes an excellent summary of man's image:

Read: 1 Thessalonians 5:23
Describe the three (3) aspects of the image of mankind:

The Word tells us we were made in God's image/likeness. What, then, is the image of God?

Image of Man = Image of God

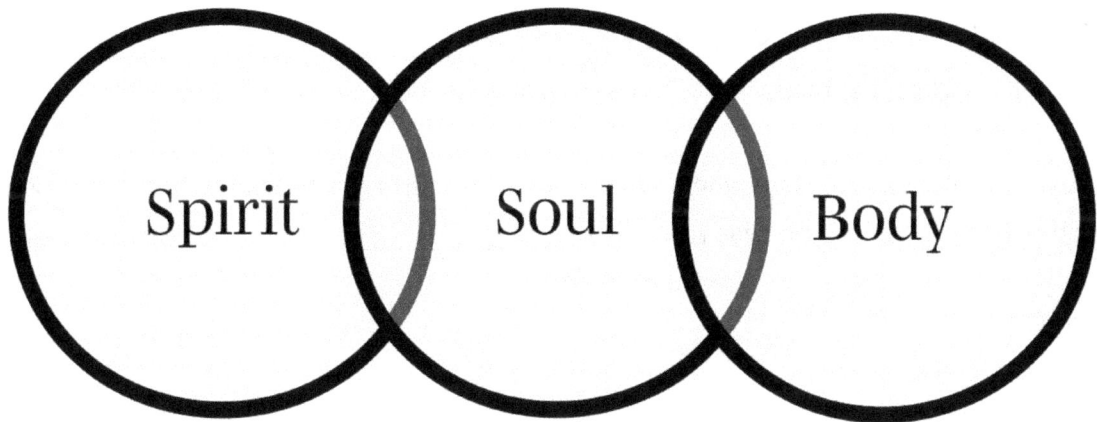

Spirit   Soul   Body

Despite being thousands of years apart, the relationship between the first couple to walk the Earth has a striking parallel to God and His Heavenly Bride, the Church of the end times. Let us explore further.

Fill in the blanks for these key passages:

REVELATION 19:6-9 (NIV)

Then I heard what sounded like a great _____, like the roar of rushing waters and like loud peals of thunder, shouting: "Hallelujah! For our Lord God Almighty reigns. Let us rejoice and be glad and give Him glory! For the _____ of the _____ has come, and His _____ has made herself ready. Fine linen, bright and clean, was given _____ to wear."

Read John 19:23-34 (on the crucifixion of Christ).

On the following page, contrast the relationship of Adam and Eve to Christ and the Church:

Eve was Adam's _____. Likewise, the Church is Christ's
_____.

Eve was created from Adam's *side*; likewise, Christ's _____ was pierced, shedding His redeeming blood and water—allowing for the creation of the Church.

Contrast Adam's physical state when Eve was created with Christ's state when the way for the Church was formed: Adam was in a deep _____. Likewise, Christ was _____ (type of sleep).

CONCLUSION:

This study established insight into the image of mankind. Since man was created in God's image, we can infer that God likewise has a spirit (John 4:24), and God has a body and a soul. When the Bible states that Adam was created in the image of God, you learned that it is not referring to the anatomy of a man. Rather, the image of mankind is clearly summarized in 1 Thessalonians 5:23 as being:

- Spirit
- Soul
- Body

SPIRIT:

Some theologians describe the spirit as part of our image that belongs to God and longs to commune with God. Upon death, the spirit returns to God (Ecclesiastes 12:7). Our spirit can feel emotions and can affect our mood and emotional state. It longs to live in communication with God. Our spirit becomes alive through the infilling of the Holy Spirit. Once alive, it requires nourishment.

SOUL:

Our soul is eternal and will abide forever in a state of life or death. The soul can be thought of as the control center of a person—where thought and reason originate and where decisions/choices are made within the bounds of free will that God has granted everyone.

BODY:

Our bodies are wonderfully created and are marvelous in many ways. It is a temporary house for the soul and spirit. Our bodies have desires—some good, some bad. Unfortunately, we inherited a sinful, carnal nature that is passed down to all (see Romans 5:12 and Romans 3:23).

We also established that God granted mankind free will. As we will learn in further studies, Adam and Eve disobeyed God's only commandment; they ate of the forbidden fruit from the tree of the knowledge of good and evil. As we consider the image of man (spirit, soul, and body), and that we are created in the image of God, we can then comprehend the possibility of developing a close and intimate relationship with God. This relationship is built on the highest form of love (*agape*).

On a corporate level, the Church is a type of bride. Collectively, we are the Bride of Christ. Just as Adam was put into a deep sleep before Eve was created from his side, likewise, Christ died (a type of sleep). Then, His side was pierced, spilling His redeeming blood and water, which led to the creation of the Church. There are only two other accounts in the Bible where men were put into a deep sleep by God:

- Abram fell into a deep sleep when God confirmed His covenant (Genesis 15:12).
- King Saul was in pursuit of David and slept in the cave where David and his men were hiding (1 Samuel 26:12).

SELF-REFLECTION:

What are your key takeaways from this study?

How would you rate your relationship with God today? Check all that apply.

- ☐ Exploring/Seeking
- ☐ New Convert/Learning
- ☐ Committed/Established
- ☐ Serving/Contributed
- ☐ Discipling Others

What actions can you take to strengthen your relationship with God?

STUDY THREE: *Fall of Man*

OPENING PRAYER:

Heavenly Father, we humble ourselves before you and acknowledge our sins and failures. Thank you for providing us with a path to redemption through the sacrifice of your Son, Jesus Christ. As we open and study your Word, we pray for your help in understanding your truth. We pray that your everlasting Word will draw us closer to you. We give you all the praise in the Holy Name of Jesus. Amen.

INTRODUCTION:

Most people would agree that humans are not perfect; we make mistakes. During job interviews, it is not uncommon for employers to question potential candidates about their strengths, weaknesses, and what mistakes they have made in their previous employment. Questions like this can be uncomfortable for the candidates unless they have a strategy to answer them positively.

Our natural tendency when a mistake is made is to hide it and hope the mistake is not discovered. This inclination is called "sweeping it under the rug." Most of you have probably seen someone try to hide or cover up a mistake. As we will learn, this is exactly what the first humans did after they disobeyed God.

Numerous studies have been conducted on human reliability. Some studies concluded that 90% of all major accidents are caused by human error. Perhaps inevitably, Adam and Eve would eventually make a mistake.

In the previous study, we established the image of man (and the image of God) and how God created the perfect paradise (Garden of Eden) for mankind to dwell. The first man, Adam, and his wife, Eve, were given free will. However, the Bible does not state how long Adam and Eve lived in paradise before their failure. Was it a year? A thousand years? We do not know.

In this study, you will gain valuable insight into the fall of mankind and the ramifications of this fall, which separated mankind from a spiritual relationship with God.

Human error contributes to more than 90% of all major accidents.

STUDY:

In Study Two, we established the punishment for Adam and Eve's disobedience, recorded in Genesis 2:17 (KJV):

> *But of the tree of the knowledge of good and evil, thou shalt not eat of it: for in the day that thou eatest thereof thou shalt surely die.*
> *Genesis 2:17 (KJV)*

According to this Scripture, the punishment for disobedience was *immediate* (in the day) death.

Read Genesis 3:1-5

Who does the serpent represent in this passage?

What did the serpent ask Eve?

In what way did Eve's account of God's commandment differ from God's actual commandment in Genesis 2:17?

What lies did the serpent tell Eve?

Why was Eve tempted to consume the forbidden fruit?

In this account, the serpent represented Satan—the enemy of our souls. There are many questions regarding these verses that we may never answer. For example, did Eve know to whom she was speaking? If so, why did she allow the conversation to continue? Was she aware that she was flirting with sin? Or was she completely unaware of who she was entertaining?

Notice in Genesis 3:3 that Eve adds to God's commandment by stating that they were not to eat of the tree of the knowledge of good and evil, nor even to touch the fruit of the forbidden tree. God did not command that they could not touch the tree, only that they were forbidden from eating the fruit from the tree. Since the commandment was given by God to Adam *before* Eve was created, she most likely learned of God's commandment indirectly from Adam and not God. Perhaps Adam added the additional commandment regarding not touching the fruit of the tree as an additional precaution.

Satan then lied to Eve by stating that she would not die. Instead, she would be like a god and gain knowledge of good and evil. In summary, Eve's temptation from Satan was:

- Life would continue.
- She would become a god.
- She would gain knowledge.

Read Genesis 3:6-13

Recall the image of man (spirit, soul, and body): what aspect of their image died whenever they sinned and disobeyed God?

What self-awareness did Adam and Eve gain from their knowledge of good and evil?

How did Adam and Eve attempt to cover their nakedness?

Who did Adam and Eve try to pin the blame on for their sins?

Adam blamed _____ and _____. Eve blamed _____.

Read Genesis 3:14-19

What were God's curses/punishments for the serpent?

What were God's curses/punishments for the woman?

What were God's curses/punishments for the man?

What is the Messianic prophecy regarding Eve's *seed* crushing the *head* of the serpent, and the serpent striking the *heel* of Eve's *seed*?

With the fall of mankind, God proclaimed several punishments and curses. First, the serpent was cursed above all cattle, confined to crawl on its belly and eat dust. There is much speculation among theologians regarding this curse. Some believe this was a metaphorical reference to Satan being expelled from Heaven and thrown to Earth (dust). Regardless, the snake slithering in the dust is a reminder of the humiliation that Satan suffered.

The woman was punished with multiplied sorrow and pain in childbirth. Also, the relational dynamic between the man and his wife would change; there would be a conflict in the desire and dominance of the relationship. The result would be anguish rather than joy and blessing.

For the man, the ground was cursed, requiring painful work and labor to produce food. Likewise, the animal kingdom was affected, forever resulting in a new balance of nature.

Genesis 3:15 is the first Messianic prophecy in the Bible. The reference to Eve's seed in this Scripture points to the birth of a savior, Christ Jesus, who would *crush* the head of the serpent, Satan. The offspring of the woman would reign victorious over Satan and sin. However, Eve's seed would experience the pain from the serpent's strike. Jesus suffered extreme pain when He was tortured and crucified. Fortunately, this strike was not permanent; Jesus resurrected on the third day to live forevermore.

Read Genesis 3:21-24
Where did God get the skins to make the clothes for Adam and Eve?

Why did God expel Adam and Eve from the Garden of Eden?

In which direction were Adam and Eve expelled from Eden?

Biblical Concept:

West to East is moving away from God.

East to West is moving toward God.

In Genesis 3:21, we read that God made coats of skins to clothe Adam and Eve. The Bible is silent regarding where the skins came from. However, some theologians believe that God killed animals for their skins, which represented the first atonement for sins. We will reference this account whenever we study atonement in a future study. Until then, a brief definition of *atonement* may provide you with additional insight into this account. Atonement means to cover. Essentially, sins can be atoned for or covered; thus, *hiding* them from the wrath of God.

God drove Adam and Eve from the Garden of Eden to separate them from the tree of life. To keep them from re-entering, cherubim with flaming swords were placed to guard the entrance. Notice that Adam and Eve were driven from the Garden of Eden, departing through the east gate. The directions east and west are spiritually significant in God's order.

Fill in the blanks for these key passages shown below:

ROMANS 3:23 (KJV)

For _____ have _____ and come short of the glory of God.

ROMANS 5:12 (KJV)

Wherefore, as by one man _____ entered into the world, and _____ by _____; and so death passed upon _____ men, for _____ have sinned.

ROMANS 6:23 (KJV)

For the wages of _____ is _____; but the gift of God is eternal life through Jesus Christ our Lord.

How did the sin of Adam and Eve affect the entire human race?

What is the punishment for sin?

Describe the spiritual state of a person before they come to Christ:

CONCLUSION:

Consider how vastly different life for humanity would have been if only Adam and Eve had chosen to obey God. I have often wondered why they were at the forbidden tree when Satan tempted them. Surely the Garden of Eden was spacious; they could have avoided the tree completely. Perhaps curiosity drew them to the tree. The Bible is silent on how they came to be present at the forbidden tree, as recorded in Genesis, Chapter 3.

In the New Testament, temptations are categorized into three types (Refer to 1 John 2:16):

- Lust of the flesh
- Lust of the eyes
- Pride of life

Which of these temptations was used by Satan to entice Eve? Perhaps Satan appealed to all three types in the following ways:

- Lust of the flesh—Eve desired the fruit and saw that the tree was good for food.
- Lust of eyes—Eve saw that the tree was "pleasant to the eyes."
- Pride of life—Eve desired to gain wisdom and to be like God.

As punishment for their disobedience and sin, they experienced spiritual death and were separated from the tree of life and spiritual fellowship with God. Unfortunately, their sin has been perpetually passed down to all of humanity, including spiritual death. (reference Romans 5:12).

Regarding the tree of life, there are several conflicting opinions from theologians on this topic. Some believe that Adam and Eve routinely partook of the fruit from the tree of life and thus continued to live indefinitely. Others believe that Adam and Eve did not consume the fruit of the tree of life before their disobedience. Further, they lived without death before sinning. Therefore, there was no need to eat of the tree of life.

In my opinion, Adam and Eve never consumed the fruit from the tree of life, before or after their sin. If they had eaten of the fruit from *this* tree after their fall, they would have gained immortality. They would have lived forever with dead spirits. Ultimately, this would have resulted in humanity being separated from God forever without the means for Redemption. To avoid this scenario, God separated them from the tree of life.

Besides spiritual death and separation from the Garden blocking access to the tree of life, God proclaimed several curses and punishments, forever altering the balance of nature. For the woman, pain in childbirth was part of the punishment. Further, she would experience conflict in her relationship with her husband. For the man, the ground was cursed, requiring labor and struggle to survive. Without a doubt, this curse had a profound impact on the remainder of the land-dwelling wildlife that God created.

The Dispensation of Innocence thus ended with Adam and Eve's disobedience. A new age began: the Dispensation of Conscience (See Appendix C). What does the sin of Adam and Eve mean to us today? Through the actions of the first man, Adam, we have inherited the death of the spirit. Yet even as they were cast out of the Garden, God had a plan for man's Redemption and spiritual rebirth.

SELF-REFLECTION:

What new insights regarding the fall of mankind did you learn from this study?

As with Adam and Eve, we all face temptations. What temptations have you experienced recently?

What strategy do you use to overcome temptations in your life?

How would you rate your effectiveness in overcoming temptation?

- ☐ I find myself always sinning.
- ☐ Most of the time, my actions result in sin.
- ☐ Sometimes my actions result in sin.
- ☐ I hardly ever sin.
- ☐ I never sin.

STUDY FOUR: *Atonement*

OPENING PRAYER:

Heavenly Father, we humble ourselves before you and acknowledge our sins and failures. Thank you for providing us with a path to atone for our sins by the shedding of blood from your Son, Jesus Christ. As we open and study your Word, we pray for understanding and revelation. We pray that your everlasting Word will draw us closer to you. We give you all the praise in the Holy Name of Jesus. Amen.

INTRODUCTION:

Have you ever seen a pet try to hide something from its owner to avoid being caught for some infraction? I witnessed this behavior many times with our dog, Dotty. On one occasion, we ordered several pizzas for my son and his friends. When the pizzas arrived, they sat unattended on the table while the boys finished their game. By the time they finished their game, the pizzas were gone! Dotty had eaten most of the pizzas and hid the rest under the bed!

Covering up mistakes is also a common behavior among humans. Perhaps we can avoid embarrassment with no one noticing. Recall that Adam and Eve tried to hide after their disobedience in the Garden of Eden. We cannot hide our sins from God. However, God provided a way for our sins to be atoned (covered).

Maybe you have heard the term "atonement" when reading or studying the Bible. Atonement is an important concept that all Christians need to understand to fully grasp God's plan for redeeming mankind and reconciling humanity to Himself. That being said, what exactly is atonement, and how is the concept of atonement relevant to us today? The goal of this study on atonement is to provide you with a high level of understanding of God's principle and approach for dealing with the sin issue caused by Adam and Eve.

The word *atonement* comes from the Hebrew word *kapar* (sometimes spelled as *kaphar*). *Kapar* (atonement) first appears in Genesis, Chapter 6, with the account of God giving Noah the plans for the ark preceding the Great Flood. God ordered Noah to *kapar*, or atone for, the ark. Later, we will explore the significance of atoning for the ark. The definition of *kapar*/atonement is: To cover or conceal.

As we progress, it is important to recognize the difference between atoning for sin versus remitting or removing sin. In atoning for sin, the sin is merely covered or hidden from God's wrath, as opposed to being remitted or removed.

Under the law of Moses in the Old Testament, there were seven holy convocations (large gatherings of people) that were observed annually. These are recorded in Leviticus, Chapter 23. Of these, there were six feasts and one fast. The fast was the Day of Atonement, and was observed on the tenth day of the seventh month (*Tishri*) on the Hebrew calendar. See Appendix A and B for a list and details regarding these seven convocations.

Jewish history records this day, *Tishri 10th*, as the anniversary of when Moses offered the atonement sacrifice for the sin of the Israelites, which involved building and worshipping the golden calf at Mount Sinai. Note that this correlation is not established in the Bible and cannot be verified.

STUDY:

After God miraculously delivered the Israelites from 400 years of Egyptian slavery through Moses' leadership, they traveled to Mount Sinai. In Chapters 19 and 20 of Exodus, we read the account of God descending on Mount Sinai and speaking the Ten Commandments, which the Israelites agreed to obey. Later in Exodus, Chapter 24, it is recorded that Moses was called up to Mount Sinai, where he was given the Law on tablets of stone.

Read Exodus 24:16-18
How many days was Moses with God on Mount Sinai?

Read Exodus 32:1-6

What did the Israelites ask of Aaron whenever they thought that Moses was not returning?

What did Aaron build?

What proclamation did Aaron make regarding the golden image that he crafted?

It seems inconceivable that so soon after God delivered the Jewish people from Egyptian slavery, they would return to idol worship. Their deliverance had been miraculous with the manifestation of the ten plagues, followed by the parting of the Red Sea and the destruction of the Egyptian armed forces.

Then, only a short time later (50 days), at Mount Sinai, they saw the fire and smoke ascend on the mountain and heard God's voice speaking the Ten Commandments. Further, they committed to obeying the Ten Commandments, including the first two found in Exodus, which state:

> *You shall have no other gods before me;*
> *You shall not make for yourself an image (idol) in the form of anything*
> *in Heaven above or on the earth beneath or in the waters below.*
> Exodus 20:3-4 *(NIV)*

Fill in the blanks for these key passages:

EXODUS 32:19 (NIV)

When Moses approached the camp and saw the _____ and the _____, his anger burned and he threw the tablets out of his hands, breaking them to pieces at the foot of the mountain.

EXODUS 32:30 (NIV)

The next day, Moses said to the people. "You have committed a great _____. But now I will go up to the Lord; perhaps I can make _____ for your sin."

What action did Moses take to address the Israelites' sin?

_____

_____

God gave Moses the plans for the Tabernacle—including the details for the Brazen Altar (Exodus Chapter 27).

EXODUS 30:10 (NIV)

Once a year Aaron shall make _____ on its horns. This annual atonement must be made with the _____ of the atoning sin offering for the generations to come. It is most holy to the Lord.

God's principle of requiring the shedding of blood as atonement for sin was formalized with the giving of the law at Mount Sinai. However, with the fall of Adam and Eve, we see traces of evidence suggesting that atonement began with the first sin. Recall that God made garments of skin to clothe Adam and Eve (Genesis 3:21).

As recorded in Exodus 30:10, Aaron (high priest of the tribe of Levi) made an atonement once a year for the sins of the nation of Israel. Sacrificial animals were slain on the Brazen Altar, shedding their blood, which was required for the atonement ritual. What was accomplished through the annual atonement ritual? The sins of the nation of Israel were atoned for or "covered." Thus, they were hidden from the wrath of God. Because the sins were only covered and not remitted, they were *rolled forward*, requiring the atonement ritual to be repeated annually.

> *For the life of the flesh is in the blood: and I have given it to you upon the altar*
> *to make an atonement for your souls: for it is the blood*
> *that maketh an atonement for your soul.*
> Leviticus 17:11 (KJV)

Read Leviticus 23:26-32 and Leviticus 1:3

When was the Day of Atonement (the Hebrew month and day)?

What was required of the Israelites on the Day of Atonement?

What happened to individuals who did not observe the Day of Atonement? And why?

Sacrifices were required to be male and without blemish.

Jewish historians believe that Tishri 10th also aligns with Ezekiel's vision of the third temple (Reference Ezekiel chapter 40). While the Levitical High Priest was performing the atonement rituals in the Tabernacle, the Israelites were required to fast (the scripture text states: "afflict themselves") and refrain from work. Those who did not honor and observe these requirements were *cut off* from their people.

While this may seem harsh, consider what the non-conformant person was declaring. By not observing the Day of Atonement, that person's sins were not atoned for or covered from the wrath of God; the judgment of God was upon them.

> *For the wages of sin is death; but the gift of God is eternal life*
> *through Jesus Christ our Lord.*
> *Romans 6:23 (KJV)*

Fill in the blanks for this key passage:

HEBREWS 9:22 (KJV)

And almost all things are by the law purged with _____; and without shedding of _____ is no remission.

Read Hebrews 10:1-4

Why were the blood sacrifices in the Old Testament offered year after year?

_____

_____

Why was it not possible for the blood of bulls and goats to take away sin?

Read Hebrews 10:5-12

Why was God not pleased with the animal blood sacrifices under the Levitical law?

In verse 9, what is the first thing He is taking away?

What is the second thing that He is establishing?

Why are animal blood sacrifices no longer required to atone for sins?

If the Old Testament saints' sins were only atoned for, when were they finally remitted?

Jesus became the human sacrifice for the sins of all humanity.

Read Romans 5:12-19

Who was the one man who caused sin to enter the world?

_____

_____

In verse 19, who was the one who made many righteous?

_____

_____

Fill in the blanks for this key passage:

Death was passed to _____ men, for _____ have sinned.

CONCLUSION:

In this study, we have only skimmed the surface of the vast subject of atonement. The goal was not to make each of you an authority on this subject, but for you to gain a high-level understanding of atonement. For one's sins to be covered (atoned), God requires the shedding of blood, which was symbolically practiced in the Old Testament times with the animal sacrifices. Essentially, God's punishment for sin is death and atonement through the shedding of blood. Further, the sacrifice was required to be a male without blemish (or imperfection, e.g., perfect).

We read in Hebrews, Chapter 10, that God did not desire the sacrifices of bulls and goats; these sacrifices did not please Him. By the grace and mercy of God, He allowed these animal sacrifices as a substitution. Why was it not possible for these animal sacrifices to take away (remit) sins? The answer becomes obvious whenever we consider *who* the offending party was. Was it the animals that sinned? No, the human race was the offending party. Therefore, the only acceptable blood sacrifice that would satisfy God's penalty for sin was a perfect human, without blemish or sin.

This study established that *all* of humanity inherited spiritual death from Adam. Therefore, there could never be a descendant of Adam who was without blemish (sin). Where then would a sinless, perfect human come from who was qualified to die and appease God's wrath for the sins of humanity? In the midst of our own inadequacy, God's plan was already in motion.

Whenever we consider the origin of Jesus, we learn that His Father was not a descendant of Adam. Rather, the Holy Spirit overshadowed Mary, and she conceived a son. Therefore, Jesus did not inherit the sinful nature from Adam.

Unlike the rest of humanity, Jesus did not have an inherent propensity for sin. However, I believe He had free will just like every human being. Even though Jesus was tempted just as we all are, He never sinned (Reference: 2 Corinthians 5:21; He knew no sin).

For us today, living in the Dispensation of Grace, only the blood of Jesus can atone for our sins once and for all. How is the blood of Jesus applied to our lives to atone for our sins? We will learn later how this is accomplished during the repentance process.

But what about the Old Testament saints of old, whose sins were atoned for by the animal sacrifices? We have established that their sins were atoned but not remitted. The Bible records in 1 Peter 3:19 and Ephesians 4:9-10 that Christ descended into Hades (or the lower parts of the earth) after his death and preached to captive spirits. Although there are conflicting views among theologians regarding these scriptures, I believe that the deceased Old Testament saints were given an opportunity to accept the Gospel of Christ, thereby having their sins remitted. Christ ultimately died and shed his blood for the entire human race. He died for those who lived before the death of Jesus on the cross, and those who lived after Jesus' sacrifice.

SELF-REFLECTION:

What new information did you gain from this study?

How do you feel knowing Jesus died and shed His blood for your sins?

STUDY FIVE: *The Gospel of Jesus Christ*

OPENING PRAYER:

Heavenly Father, we thank you for the good news of the Gospel of Jesus Christ. Thank you for the hope of eternal life through Jesus Christ. We open our minds and our hearts to receive your Word. Let understanding and new revelations come to each of us through this study. May your Word strengthen our faith and trust in you. We give you all the praise in the Holy Name of Jesus. Amen.

INTRODUCTION:

I remember the day we learned that my wife was expecting our first child. We were so full of joy and excitement with the good news! Whenever I informed my parents, they were overwhelmed with emotion. Mother was crying, Dad was laughing, and both were thrilled to learn that they were going to be grandparents. I'm guessing you've all had similar moments when sharing exciting news with family and friends.

Although the news that we were expecting our first child was good news, it did not come close in comparison to the good news of the Gospel of Jesus Christ. I hope and pray that this study will inspire you with the good news of the Gospel. May it be such that you become enthusiastic about sharing the Gospel with all who are open to hearing.

In previous studies, we established that God created mankind in His own image. Mankind and God have a spirit, soul, and body. Then, we studied the fall of man and the resulting spiritual death. We learned how sin and death are passed on to all of humanity. Now you have a general understanding of God's punishment for sin and God's principle of atonement. I want to turn your attention now towards God's plan for redeeming mankind.

Understanding God's plan for redemption begins with a study of the Gospel of Jesus Christ. The word *gospel* is a Greek word that means *good news*. In the Bible, the Gospel of Jesus Christ is a specific pattern of events. As you will learn in future studies in this book, this Gospel pattern is repeated symbolically through several events recorded in the Bible.

Jesus' ministry lasted only three and a half years, but it permanently impacted the world!

STUDY:

Fill in the blanks for this key passage:

1 CORINTHIANS 15:1-4 (KJV)

Moreover, brethren, I declare unto you the _____ which I preached unto you, which also ye have received, and wherein you stand; By which also ye are _____, if ye keep in memory what I preached unto you, unless ye have believed in vain. For I delivered unto you first of all that which I also received, how that Christ _____ for our sins according to the scriptures; And that He was _____, and that He _____ again the third day according to the scriptures.

According to these scriptures, what is the Gospel of Jesus Christ?

_____

_____

One of the most passionate preachers of the Gospel was the Apostle Paul. In Paul's first letter to the Church at Corinth, he declares to them the Gospel which he had previously preached to them. The Gospel of Jesus Christ is declared as the *death, burial*, and *resurrection*. Further, Paul describes that he is passing on the Gospel truth that he received. From whom did Paul receive this truth? In Galatians 1:12, we learn that Paul received this revelation directly from Jesus, and not from man.

For those interested in learning more, I encourage you to study Paul's conversion from Judaism to Christianity (see Acts, Chapter 9). As you read, you notice that Paul's given name was Saul (a Hebrew name). Saul used his Greek name, *Paul*, after his conversion; he did not want to be associated with his past life. What a remarkable transformation!

It was several years after Paul's conversion before he met with the apostles at Jerusalem. He ensured his Gospel message aligned with those of the apostles (reference Galatians chapters 1 and 2). The point being, Paul received the revelation of the Gospel of Jesus Christ independently, and not from men. However, Paul's revelation of the Gospel matched that of the other apostles, which is an amazing testament to the consistency of the Gospel.

—JESUS TOOK ON THE SINS OF HUMANITY—

Fill in the blanks for this key passage:

2 CORINTHIANS 5:21 (NIV)

God made Him [Jesus] who had no _____ to be _____ for _____, so that in Him [**Jesus**] _____ might become the righteousness of God. (*Note: Highlighted name added for clarity.*)

Under the law of Moses, the priest would lay his hands on the head of the sacrificial animal (reference Leviticus 4:24). By doing so, the sins were symbolically transferred onto the sacrifice, which was then slain on the Brazen Altar. The sin was being punished by the death of the sacrifice and the shedding of its blood.

Recall our study of atonement. Just as the sacrificial animals under the Mosaic law were innocent and without blemish, likewise, Jesus was innocent and without sin. In both cases, the sacrificial animals and the innocent human (Jesus) took on the sins, then died and shed their blood for the atonement of sins.

The Gospel of Jesus Christ is: Death, Burial and Resurrection

—THE DEATH OF JESUS CHRIST—

Each of the four Gospels (Matthew, Mark, Luke, and John) contains an account of the death of Jesus. Although they offer similar accounts, each adds a different perspective and level of detail. Taken together, we can gain a deeper insight into the details surrounding the crucifixion of Jesus.

When reading the scriptures related to the crucifixion, refer to Appendix E for details on the Hebrew Day. During daylight hours, the sundial was used; 7 a.m., our time, was the first hour of the day. Noon was the sixth hour of the day, etc.

Read the scriptures (KJV) listed in the table below and which carry over to the next page. Mark the boxes if the text contains the details listed.

SCRIPTURE DETAILS	MATTHEW 27:32-52	MARK 15:21-38	LUKE 23:26-46	JOHN 19:17-30
Simon carried His cross.				
The location of the crucifixion was Golgotha.				
Soldiers cast lots for His clothes.				
Jesus forgives the soldiers for crucifying Him.				

SCRIPTURE DETAILS	MATTHEW 27:32-52	MARK 15:21-38	LUKE 23:26-46	JOHN 19:17-30
Sign: THIS IS JESUS, THE KING OF THE JEWS				
Sign: THE KING OF THE JEWS				
Sign: THIS IS THE KING OF THE JEWS				
Sign: JESUS OF NAZARETH, THE KING OF THE JEWS				
Crucified at the third hour of the day.				
Darkness from the sixth hour to the ninth hour.				
Christ died at the ninth hour.				
Christ's side was pierced; blood and water flowed.				
Christ's legs were not broken.				
Earthquakes occurred.				
Veil in the Temple torn from top to bottom.				
Rocks rent.				
Graves opened.				

Notice the text contains some variation. For example, the details regarding the sign over the crucified Christ are slightly different. These are not contradictions, but each writer recorded a different level of detail in their account. The crucifixion of Christ began at the third hour of the day (9 a.m.). Darkness came on the land beginning at the sixth hour of the day (noon) and lasted until His death, which occurred at the ninth hour of the day (3 p.m.).

After His death, His side was pierced. His blood became the ultimate means for the atonement of the sins of mankind. Some theologians believe the water that came from His side is a type and shadow of water baptism. The crucifixion of Christ occurred on a Friday, the next day being a Sabbath and the Passover.

Therefore, there was an urgency to complete the crucifixions and bury the bodies before the end of the day (6 p.m.). To expedite matters, the soldiers would break the legs of the condemned, thus preventing them from *pushing* up to take another breath. However, whenever they came to Jesus, they found Him already dead, fulfilling the prophecy that His bones would not be broken (Psalms 34:20).

—THE BURIAL OF JESUS CHRIST—

Read the scriptures (KJV) listed in the table below and on the next page. Mark the boxes if the text contains the details listed.

SCRIPTURE DETAILS	MATTHEW 27:57-61	MARK 15:42-47	LUKE 23:50-56	JOHN 19:38-42
Joseph of Arimathea asked Pilate for the body of Jesus.				
Pilate checked with the centurion to know that Jesus was dead.				
Pilate gave Jesus' body to Joseph.				
Joseph took Jesus' body.				
Joseph wrapped Jesus' body in a linen cloth.				
Joseph laid Jesus' body in his own tomb.				
Joseph laid Jesus' body in a sepulcher hewn from rock.				

SCRIPTURE DETAILS	MATTHEW 27:57-61	MARK 15:42-47	LUKE 23:50-56	JOHN 19:38-42
Joseph laid Jesus' body in a sepulcher; never had a man been laid.				
Nicodemus brought myrrh and aloes to anoint the body.				
They rolled a great stone over the door of the tomb.				
The tomb was in a garden near where Jesus was crucified.				
Mary Magdalene and another Mary were at the tomb.				
The Sabbath was the following day.				

As we study the four different accounts of Jesus' burial, various details come to light that provide us with key insight. In an upcoming study of the Passover, I will present further details regarding the death, burial, and resurrection of Christ. For now, it is important to understand that Jesus died on a Friday; the next day was the seventh day of the week, the Sabbath. Further, the next day was also the Passover, which was a significant holiday and holy convocation for the Jewish people.

In keeping with the Jewish tradition and laws, the Jews could not work on the Sabbath. Moving, preparing, and burying the body of Jesus would have been prohibited. There was an urgency by Joseph (and perhaps Nicodemus) to collect the body of Jesus and complete the burial before 6 p.m. (12th hour of the day). They made a quick decision to use Joseph's tomb, which was in the garden close to Golgotha, the crucifixion site.

Mark's account tells us that Pilate was surprised that Jesus was already dead and called for the centurion to confirm His death before releasing the body to Joseph. The body of Jesus was then prepared with a linen wrap and anointed with spices provided by Nicodemus. Afterward, they buried Him in Joseph's tomb, where no man had ever been buried. Once the burial was complete, they rolled a heavy stone over the door of the tomb and departed.

Several of the accounts record two women being present and witnessing the burial. Since the following day after His burial was the Sabbath, there was no activity recorded on that day other than the women preparing spices to anoint His body. Finally, we can assume from the accounts that the guards remained on duty after His burial and until after His resurrection.

—THE RESURRECTION OF JESUS CHRIST—

Read the scriptures (KJV) listed in the table below and on the following pages. Mark the boxes if the text contains the details listed in the box.

SCRIPTURE DETAILS	MATTHEW 27:62- 28:6	MARK 16:1-7	LUKE 24:1-8	JOHN 20:1-2
The Pharisees asked Pilate to guard the tomb.				
Mary Magdalene and Mary came to the tomb on the first day of the week.				
There was a great earthquake.				
The angel of the Lord descended and rolled back the stone.				
The angel sat upon the stone.				
The angel's countenance was like lightning with a white garment.				

SCRIPTURE DETAILS	MATTHEW 27:62- 28:6	MARK 16:1-7	LUKE 24:1-8	JOHN 20:1-2
The guards were fearful and shook; they became as dead men.				
Mary and Mary brought spices to anoint the body.				
The women wondered who would roll away the stone for them.				
The stone was already rolled away when the women arrived.				
Women entered the sepulcher and saw a young man in white.				
Two men in shining garments stood by the women.				
Women were frightened at the sight of the young man.				
He asked: Why seek the living among the dead?				
He said: Be not afraid, the crucified Jesus of Nazareth is risen.				
He said: He is not here; behold the place where they laid Him.				

SCRIPTURE DETAILS	MATTHEW 27:62- 28:6	MARK 16:1-7	LUKE 24:1-8	JOHN 20:1-2
He said: Go quickly and tell His disciples; He is risen.				
He said: Tell His disciples and Peter that He goes before you.				
He said: You will see Him in Galilee, as He said unto you.				
He said: Remember, He said, the Son of Man must be delivered into the hands of sinful men, and be crucified, and the third day rise again.				
The women remembered the words of Jesus.				

A detailed view of the discovery of Jesus' resurrection takes shape as we compare these four accounts side-by-side. First, we read of the two women, Mary Magdalene and Mary, arriving at the tomb early on Sunday morning. They had with them spices to anoint the body of Jesus. Yet they wondered how they would access the body since a heavy stone was blocking the entrance.

Whenever they arrived, there were two angels present, but only one angel spoke to the women. One account provides specific details regarding an angel descending from Heaven and rolling away the heavy stone. I can only imagine the fear that those guarding the tomb must have felt when the angel descended and rolled back the heavy stone. If this was not frightful enough for them, the earthquake occurring at the same moment must have been overwhelming. It is no wonder that they fell down as dead men, probably in a fainting spell brought on by their extreme fear.

As we study the various accounts recorded, we learn the details of the conversation between the angel and the women. The women discover the resurrection of Jesus and leave to tell His disciples.

CONCLUSION:

The life, death, burial, and resurrection of Jesus were the most significant events in the history of planet Earth. For the first and only time, a perfect man resurrected from the dead, by His own power, to live forevermore. While there were a few examples of Jesus raising the dead to life during His ministry, those individuals eventually expired just as all men are appointed to die. Jesus, and He alone, defeated death.

Some doubt the account of Jesus' resurrection. However, if a person is truly open to the truth, there is overwhelming evidence of His resurrection. Consider how awesome God's love is for humanity—that the Creator of the universe would robe Himself in flesh. He became part of His Creation. He then endured the punishment for the sins of man by becoming the perfect human sacrifice, without blemish.

History records the death of Jesus as occurring on Friday, Nisan 14th, AD 33 (Hebrew calendar). His resurrection thus occurred on Sunday, Nisan 16th, AD 33. This date also marks the date of the Feast of First Fruits. On this day, the Israelites would take a sample (first fruits) of their crops before harvest and present it to the priest. The priest would inspect the first fruits and, if accepted, he would offer the first fruits to God with a wave offering. Once the first fruits were blessed by God, the remainder of the crop was likewise considered blessed. The concept of the first fruits was a typology of the work of Jesus Christ at Calvary. See Leviticus 23:9-14 and Deuteronomy 26:1-12 for details.

According to 1 Corinthians 15:20-24, Jesus' sacrifice became the first fruit. God inspected the work of Jesus, His death, burial, and resurrection. God saw that Jesus' work was acceptable and blessed His work (first fruits). Therefore, all who come after Jesus are likewise blessed.

What does this mean for us today? Through Christ, we can have the hope of eternal life and someday experience resurrection to live forevermore with our Lord and Savior, Jesus Christ.

The Good News: Jesus died for our sins. Jesus was buried.

Jesus was resurrected. He is alive forevermore!

SELF-REFLECTION:

Rank the four authors of the Gospels (Matthew, Mark, Luke, and John) by the level of detail provided in their written accounts of the Gospel.

LEVEL OF DETAIL	MATTHEW	MARK	LUKE	JOHN
Most detailed				
2nd Most detailed				
3rd Most detailed				
Least detailed				

What new information did you gain from this study?

Of the Scriptures read in this study, which one had the biggest impact on you?

STUDY SIX: *Obeying the Gospel*

OPENING PRAYER:

Heavenly Father, we thank you for the good news of the Gospel of Jesus Christ. We humble ourselves before you and desire to live in obedience to your Word. We open our minds and our hearts to receive your Word and pray for understanding as we study the Bible. May we be strengthened and blessed as we submit our hearts to your will. We give you all the praise in the Holy Name of Jesus. Amen.

INTRODUCTION:

In the last study, we established that the Gospel of Jesus Christ was the good news of His death, burial, and resurrection. Indeed, what great news for those who commit their lives to Christ Jesus and obey His Gospel; they will inherit eternal life.

Christian religious denominations today offer a wide range of views and doctrines regarding the application of the Gospel of Jesus Christ for one to achieve salvation. My goal with this study is to establish the Biblical approach to obeying the Gospel for salvation. That being said, this approach may conflict with some religious doctrines. However, the goal is not to convert anyone away from their religious affiliation. I hope and pray that you will approach this study with an open mind, laying aside preconceived thoughts on this subject.

I will reconcile several scriptures that are sometimes used to argue for a *minimal* approach to salvation. Such scriptures appear to be contradictions in the Biblical text. Typically, in my experience, these situations occur because of the various English translations available to us. For example, some Hebrew and Greek words do not have a "one-to-one" word translation in English.

However, those translating the Biblical text sometimes chose a single word for the English translation, resulting in the loss of the full meaning.

For any additional scriptures used to justify your approach to salvation not included in my reconciliation, please explore independently of this study. If you do not own an interlinear Bible to reference, several free online versions are available to you.

Two of my standard references are:

blueletterBible.org   scripture4all.org

STUDY:

Fill in the blanks for these key passages:

2 THESSALONIANS 1:8 (KJV)

In flaming fire, taking _____ on them that know not God, and that _____ not the Gospel of our Lord Jesus Christ.

1 PETER 4:17 (KJV)

For the time is come that _____ must begin at the house of God: and if it first begins with us, what shall the end be of them that _____ not the gospel of God?

What will the punishment be for those who do *not* obey the Gospel?

Here's a rhetorical question:

Since the Gospel is the death, burial, and resurrection of Jesus,

how can one obey the Gospel?

The rhetorical question above can be both engaging and challenging. Hopefully and prayerfully, this question has captivated your interest and attention! Before we establish the answer to this thought-provoking question, let's explore the historical event of the outpouring of the Holy Spirit on the Day of Pentecost.

Read Acts 2:1-8

What appeared and sat upon each of them gathered there?

What happened to those who received the Holy Spirit?

Why were the Jews from foreign nations confounded (or bewildered)?

The outpouring of the Holy Spirit in this text ushered in a new dispensation of time: the Dispensation of Grace (See Appendix C). At this event, Jews from all around the world had gathered in Jerusalem for the Feast of Pentecost, which was one of the seven convocations established in chapter 23 of Leviticus. (See Appendix A and B.) They were amazed when they heard local Galileans speaking in their native language. They knew that those speaking did not know the languages in which they spoke. If you are not familiar with this event, I would encourage you to read and study the entire chapter of Acts 2.

Later in Acts, Chapter 2, Peter, one of the 12 disciples, preached the first Apostolic message to the crowd gathered that day. The message became the foundation on which the early Christian church was founded. But where did Peter get his authority to establish the early Christian church?

Read Matthew 16:13-19
What was Peter's revelation regarding who Jesus was?

As we seek to grasp the full meaning of Jesus' words in Matthew 16:18, it is beneficial to examine the Greek words for "Peter" and "rock." The root word for "Peter" is *Petros*, which means movable stone, pebble, or small rock. However, the word for "rock" in this verse is *petra*, which means a large, massive rock. Use the QR code here to find out more.

Considering these definitions and the context of Matthew 16:18 relative to the preceding verses (15-17), it becomes clear that Jesus was stating that Peter (Petros) would have a part to play in the kingdom of God. However, the church that Jesus would build would be built on the "large rock" (petra).

The rock was Peter's revelation that Jesus was the Christ! Jesus Christ Himself is the chief cornerstone.

What, then, is the rock (*petra*) that Jesus would build His church upon?

What keys did Jesus give to Peter?

Jesus asked His disciples who they thought He was. Peter answered: "You are the Christ, the Son of the Living God."

Jesus blessed Peter and stated, "Upon this *rock* I will build my Church." The *rock* is the revelation that Jesus was the Christ.

In verse 19 of Matthew, Chapter 16, Jesus gave Peter the "keys to the kingdom." Peter probably did not fully comprehend the significance of this statement. Essentially, Jesus authorized Peter to establish the early Church.

Peter, with the authority given by Jesus Himself, established how to obey the Gospel for salvation. Towards the end of Peter's apostolic message recorded in this chapter, the Bible states in Acts 2:37 that those listening were "pricked in their hearts." They asked Peter and the disciples, "What shall we do?"

Peter's response is a concise pattern for the rhetorical question posed on page 63, "How do we obey the Gospel?"

Fill in the blanks for this key passage:

ACTS 2:38-39 (KJV)

Then Peter said unto them, _____, and be _____ every one of you in the _____ of _____ _____ for the remission of sins, and ye shall receive the gift of the Holy Ghost. For the _____ is unto you, and to your children, and to all that are afar off, even as many as the Lord our God shall call.

—REPENTANCE (TYPOLOGY OF DEATH)—

In the Bible, repentance is much more than just having Godly sorrow for our sins. Repentance is also to turn from a sinful lifestyle and turn towards a Godly lifestyle; repentance is destroying sin from our lives. Let's explore *repentance* from a Biblical perspective.

Fill in the blanks for this key passage:

2 PETER 3:9 (NIV)

The Lord is not slow in keeping His promise, as some understand slowness. He is patient with you, not wanting anyone to _____, but everyone to come to _____.

What does this Scripture imply will happen to those who do not repent?

Fill in the blanks for this key passage:

ROMANS 6:6 (KJV)

Knowing this, that our old man is _____ with Him, that the body of _____ might be _____ that henceforth, we should not serve _____.

Which of the three commandments in Peter's message (Acts 2:38) is being described in Romans 6:6?

Is repentance essential for salvation?

As we have established in these scriptures, *repentance is essential for salvation* and one of the first steps that a new believer must take. Repentance was a common theme in the New Testament, where it is discussed in over 40 accounts. The theme of repentance started with John the Baptist (see Synoptic Gospels), when he preached, "Repent, for the kingdom of God is at hand," in Matthew 3:2 (NIV). Likewise, Jesus also preached repentance (See Matthew 4:17). It should come as no surprise that Peter's first apostolic message on the Day of Pentecost included the commandment to repent (See Acts 2:38). Other scriptures, for example, 2 Peter 3:9 and Romans 6:6, support the conclusion that repentance is indeed essential for salvation.

The terminology the writer uses in Romans 6:6 relates repentance to death, e.g., crucifixion of the old man (referencing our carnal, sinful nature).

—BAPTISM (TYPOLOGY OF BURIAL)—

Another step in obeying the Gospel of Jesus Christ is being baptized in the name of Jesus Christ. The word "baptize" comes from the Greek word *bapto,* which means *to dip or immerse.* We have established that Peter was given the keys to the kingdom of Heaven. On the Day of Pentecost, Peter commanded the people gathered to be baptized in the name of Jesus Christ for the remission of sins. (found in Acts 2). We will now further explore Biblical baptism by looking at important verses.

Fill in the blanks for these key passages:

MARK 16:16 (KJV)

He that believeth and is _____ shall be saved; but he that believeth not shall be _____.

According to this scripture, is Baptism essential for salvation?

_____

_____

ROMANS 6:3-4 (KJV)

Know ye not, that so many of us as were _____ into Jesus Christ were baptized into His _____? Therefore we are _____ with Him by _____ into death: that like as Christ was raised from the dead by the glory of the Father, even so we also should walk in newness of life.

How is one's baptism related to the burial of Jesus Christ?

_____

_____

COLOSSIANS 2:12 (KJV)

_____ with Him in _____, wherein also ye are risen with Him through the faith of the operation of God, who hath raised Him from the dead.

Whenever a person is baptized, with whom are they symbolically being buried?

_____

_____

These scriptures confirm that *baptism is essential for salvation*. Baptism is another step in obeying the Gospel of Jesus Christ by being symbolically buried with him. Being immersed in water is a type and shadow of being buried. Being baptized in Jesus Christ's name is a symbolic burial with Him.

THE PATTERN OF REDEMPTION- 69

Whenever we repent of our sins and are baptized in the name of Jesus Christ, our sins are washed away (removed or remitted).

—RECEIVING THE HOLY SPIRIT (TYPOLOGY OF RESURRECTION)—

Read John 3:1-6

What two births must take place before a person can enter the kingdom of God?

How is a person "born of the spirit?"

Although Nicodemus was confused by Jesus' comments as recorded in John chapter 3, today we have the benefit of the New Testament, which reveals God's pattern of redemption. Being born of the Spirit occurs whenever a person receives the gift of the Holy Spirit from God. Once a person does their part to obey the Gospel of Jesus Christ, then God offers them the gift of the Holy Spirit.

As the obedient believer receives and accepts this gift, their spirit experiences the spiritual birth that Jesus foretold to Nicodemus. By receiving the Holy Spirit, our spirit becomes alive through the new birth process. We will explore the gift of the Holy Spirit in more detail later in this book.

—SCRIPTURE RECONCILIATION—

Some of you who may ask, "But what about John 3:16, etc.? Doesn't this scripture and other similar scriptures contradict what we studied regarding obeying the Gospel?" In my search for the truth, I discovered this apparent contradiction to be an issue with the Greek-to-English translation of the Biblical text.

Read John 3:16

In the Greek text, the word *pisteuo* is used, and was translated into English as *believe*. However, not all words in other languages can be translated into a single word in English. Sometimes, the definitions are much broader than a single word can describe. Such is the case with *pisteuo*. According to the Greek Lexicon dictionary, the word *pisteuo* means: believe, commit, entrust, adhere, and obey.

Considering this broader definition, John 3:16 is therefore implying that salvation is available to those who not only believe but also commit, entrust, adhere, and obey. Clearly, more is required for salvation according to the Greek text in John 3:16 than simply a mental ascent of believing.

I have referenced a few sources below. However, many additional sources provide the same conclusion. For those skeptical, I suggest conducting additional searches to confirm this information.

Read Acts 2:21

In the Greek text, the word *epikaleo* was translated as *shall call on* in the English translation of this scripture. The definition of *epikaleo* means: call on; be surnamed; to take on the name of (as in a marriage), to permit oneself to be surnamed; to be named after someone.

Now that we understand the broader meaning of this scripture, more is required than just calling out the name of Jesus. Taking on His name, as in a marriage, is much more involved. How does one take on the name of Jesus? Galatians 3:27 states that when one is baptized into Christ, they "put on" Christ.

BlueletterBible.org "Pisteuo"	Wordpress.com Definition of "pisteuo"	Billmouncer.com Definition of "pisteuo"

BlueletterBible.org Definition of "Epikaleo"	BlueletterBible.org "Epikaleo"

CONCLUSION:

It is humbling to consider the depth of love that God has for humanity. A love that motivated Him to send His only begotten Son into this world as a sacrifice, to die for our sins. In doing so, He paid the ultimate penalty for the sins of humanity and made a way to reconcile us to Himself. Now, through obedience to the Gospel, we can have salvation and the hope of eternal life with Christ Jesus.

May every person who finishes this study clearly understand the pattern of God's salvation plan. This pattern directly aligns with the Gospel of Jesus Christ:

- **Jesus died—We must die**; not a physical death, but through repentance, which is symbolic of crucifying one's carnal, sinful nature.
- **Jesus was buried—We must be buried**; not in a physical sense, but symbolically through baptism in the name of Jesus.
- **Jesus resurrected—We must be resurrected** by receiving the Holy Spirit, which is the *new birth* of our spirit within us. Before receiving the Holy Spirit, our spirit was dead through sin (See Ephesians 2:1).

The following table will be developed further as you progress through this book:

GOSPEL	DEATH	BURIAL	RESURRECTION
Jesus	Crucified	Buried	Rose again on the 3rd day
Believer Obeying the Gospel	Repents Dying of the Carnal Nature	Baptized Buried with Christ Jesus	Receives the Holy Spirit Spiritual Birth

The goal with this table is to assist you in understanding the correlation between the Gospel of Jesus Christ and our obedience to the Gospel. This pattern is repeated symbolically and in types/shadows through the Old Testament:

- Death/Repentance
- Burial/Baptism, and
- Resurrection/Receiving the Holy Spirit

Upcoming studies will provide a more detailed look at a few of these.

SELF-REFLECTIONS:

What aspect of the study on *Obeying the Gospel* affected you the most?

Where do you currently find yourself on your spiritual journey?

- ☐ Interested and Learning
- ☐ New Believer and Growing
- ☐ In a Repentance Process
- ☐ Fully Repented
- ☐ Baptized in Jesus' Name
- ☐ Have Received the Holy Spirit

Describe your plan for progressing through the steps to obey the Gospel:

STUDY SEVEN: *Noah and the Great Flood*

OPENING PRAYER:

Heavenly Father, thank you for revealing the pattern of redemption throughout the Bible. As we open your Word, we pray that this study will reveal to us your master plan for the redemption of mankind. Prepare our minds and our hearts to receive your Word as seeds that fall on good soil. May we be strengthened and blessed as we submit our hearts to your will. We give you all the praise in the Holy Name of Jesus. Amen.

INTRODUCTION:

I have lived in Southeast Texas for most of my life. After my retirement, we relocated to the Texas Hill Country. One of the major factors that influenced our move away from the flat coastal land of Texas was the threat of hurricanes. I refer to that area as the "hurricane bowling alley." Having endured one house flood was enough for me. Watching several family members lose everything they owned to Hurricane Harvey was heartbreaking. As horrific as these hurricane forces are, imagine an apocalyptic flood on a global scale.

As you will learn in this study, the account of Noah and the Great Flood is much more than just a children's story. Instead, the account of this great man (Noah) and the flood is rich in spiritual symbolism. Recall from the previous study on the Gospel of Jesus Christ, we established the pattern of the Gospel of Jesus Christ as being His death, burial, and resurrection.

With this study of Noah and the Great Flood, you will discover a repeating pattern (on a macro level) of the Gospel as we explore the Scriptures. This account is the first occurrence of this pattern in the Bible. This study also confirms the correlation between death and repentance.

Repentance is a type of death with the dying away of the carnal, sinful nature. The Scriptures in this study will confirm the correlation between burial and water baptism. It is important to understand these symbolic correlations to grasp the full understanding of the Genesis account of Noah and the flood.

I recommend that you review Genesis, Chapter 5, before beginning the study. In these scriptures, you will find the genealogy of Noah.

There were ten generations from Adam to Noah.

STUDY:

Read Genesis 6:5

How does the Bible describe the moral state of humanity in the day of Noah?

_____

_____

_____

Fill in the blanks for this key passage:

GENESIS 6:6-7 (KJV)

And it _____ the Lord that He had made man on the earth, and it grieved Him at His heart. And the Lord said, I will _____ man whom I have created from the face of the earth; both man, and beast, and the creeping thing, and the fowls of the air; for it _____ me that I have made them.

Notice the choice of words used to describe God's wrath towards the wickedness of humanity: God "repented," then destroyed sin from the world. Even though the term "repented" was translated to represent God's actions, this does *not* imply that God sinned, or that He made a mistake.

God is perfect in all of His ways and cannot sin or fail. Rather, God was so grieved because His creation had become so wicked, He chose to give us a perfect example of repentance. God's example of repentance is a model that all of us should consider whenever we sin or fail.

What action(s) did God plan whenever He demonstrated *repentance* for creating mankind?

What does it mean for us to repent of sins? Does it mean more than being sorrowful?

Read Genesis 6:8-13, Hebrews 11:7 and Romans 1:17
Why was Noah referred to as a "just man?"

What were the names of Noah's three sons?

Describe the state of humanity that was displeasing to God?

In Genesis 6:9, Noah is referred to as a "just man." Thus, he found *grace* in the eyes of the Lord (Genesis 6:8). In Hebrews 11:7 and Romans 1:17, we learn that Noah had faith in God and that the "just" shall live by faith. Keep in mind that before the Great Flood, Noah lived in the Dispensation of Conscience. The Ten Commandments did not yet exist. There was no law to follow, nor was there a Bible to read and study. Humanity then only had the knowledge of good and evil, which they inherited from their ancestor Adam.

However, there is evidence that the concept of sacrifices for atonement was probably understood. Galatians 3:6 records that belief in God was imputed as righteousness. Although this scripture is referring to Abraham, it would likewise apply to Noah, who lived before the giving of the law.

As a note of interest, Noah's three sons, Shem, Ham, and Japheth, replenished the earth after the flood as follows (See Genesis, Chapters 9, 10, and 11):

- Shem: Jews, Arabs, Asians
- Ham: Egypt, Africa
- Japheth: Europe, parts of Asia

Read Genesis 6:14-16

In verse 14, the word "pitch" in the English Bible translation is *kapar* in the Hebrew text. Recall from our previous study of atonement, *kapar* is the Hebrew word for *atonement*.

What is the spiritual typology regarding God requiring Noah to atone for the ark?

The first use of the word *kapar* in the Bible is found in Genesis 6:14. God directed Noah to atone for (i.e., cover, or hide) the ark. In doing so, those within the ark would be atoned, covered, and protected from the imminent wrath of God that was forthcoming with the flood.

Research shows that pitch back in the time of Noah was made primarily from tree sap. However, some references document that certain types of pitch in that era were created using a mixture of tree sap and animal blood. Could it have been that Noah actually atoned for the ark using this mixture with animal blood?

Unfortunately, the history has been lost over time; we do not know. Regardless, it is intriguing to consider that Noah may have used animal blood to atone for his ark, in keeping with God's principle of atonement. There are three arks mentioned in the Bible:

- Noah's ark
- Moses' ark
- The Ark of the Covenant

Of these, the ark created to hide Moses in the Nile River was also covered in pitch (see Exodus 2:3). Interestingly, the Hebrew word *zepet* is used to describe the pitch used to cover Moses' ark. Why was a different word or type of pitch used? I believe it was different because Moses' ark did not require being atoned or covered to shield Moses from the wrath of God. In this account, Moses was being hidden from the wrath of man (Pharaoh). Thus, atonement was unnecessary.

Genesis 6:15-16 features the account of the ark's design. A cubit is the length of a man's arm from his elbow to the tip of his middle finger. The average size of men in Noah's time could have been different compared to today's population. Historians can only estimate the length of a cubit by today's standards of measurement. A cubit is estimated to be 18 inches (46 centimeters) in length. Using this conversion, the ark would have been approximately 450 feet long, 75 feet wide, and 45 feet high.

How many doors were on Noah's ark?

Read Ephesians 4:5 and John 14:6
What is spiritually symbolic of the *one door* on the side of the ark?

Just as the ark had only one door, there is only one Lord, one Faith, and one Baptism. Jesus is the only way to God, and the only way to gain salvation. Noah and his family only had one option to escape the flood: to enter through the only door of the ark. Likewise, believers today only have one option for gaining salvation and the hope of eternal life; that is, through Jesus Christ and obeying His Gospel. For some Bible scholars, the side door of the ark was a type and shadow of Jesus' side being pierced during His crucifixion.

Read Genesis 6:17-22 and 1 Peter 3:20-21

The flood was a serious, life-threatening event for Noah and his family. How, then, were they "saved" by the water?

How is the Great Flood symbolic of our baptism?

How is the account of Noah and the Great Flood symbolic of the Gospel of Jesus Christ?

The Great Flood was indeed a serious, life-threatening event for Noah and his family. However, 1 Peter 3:20 states that the water saved Noah and his family. To fully understand this concept, one must consider the flood from a spiritual perspective. Remember that God repented that He had created man. God then destroyed His Creation. However, Noah and his family were saved from the wrath of God (the flood) by the ark. Noah's salvation was essentially spiritual since the sins of the world were washed away and buried by the flood.

Consider the typology of the resurrection of the human race, which occurred after the flood. Noah and his family began a new life on Earth without the influence of sin. All evidence of the wickedness of man had been washed away in the flood.

Here are some important facts to remember about the flood:

- It rained for forty days and forty nights during the Great Flood.
- The flood lasted for 371 days.
- Noah and his family were saved from the wrath of God by the atonement covering of the ark.

CONCLUSION:

It should be noted that all humans born after the flood are descendants of Noah. Whether a person has dark-colored skin or light-colored skin, blond hair or dark hair, blue eyes or brown eyes, we are all descendants of Noah.

In Genesis 9:9-12, we read the account of God's covenant with Noah (see Appendix D). This covenant ushered in a new dispensation of time: the Dispensation of Human Governance (see Appendix C). With this covenant, God promised never to destroy the world again by water and gave Noah a token; the rainbow in the sky is a reminder of His covenant.

Woven into the account of Noah and the flood are all the elements of the Gospel of Jesus Christ. First, there is *repentance*; God repented that He had created man. Then, we read of the flood, which is a type of *burial or baptism* on a macro scale. In 1 Peter 3:20-21, the Bible compares the flood, which washed away the sins of the world, to our baptism, which washes away our sins after we have repented. Last, consider the *resurrection* of humanity that occurred after the flood. Noah and his family began a new life without the influence of sin affecting their lives from immoral humanity.

Below is an updated chart showing the pattern of the Gospel that has been identified in our study of Noah:

GOSPEL	DEATH	BURIAL	RESURRECTION
Jesus	Crucified	Buried	Rose again on the 3rd day
Believer Obeying the Gospel	Repents Dying of the Carnal Nature	Baptized Buried with Christ Jesus	Receives the Holy Spirit Spiritual Birth
Noah and his Family	Repentance God repented for creating man	Burial Flood buried the Earth	Resurrection New life without sin, after the Flood

SELF-REFLECTIONS:

What fresh revelations did you gain from the study of Noah and the flood?

How does the practical information in this study apply to your spiritual walk with God?

STUDY EIGHT: *Abrahamic Covenant*

OPENING PRAYER:

Heavenly Father, thank you for the patriarchs of old and the covenants that you made with men. As we open your Word and study the Abrahamic covenant, help us grasp how this covenant applies to us today. Prepare our minds and our hearts to receive and obey your Word. May we be strengthened and blessed as we submit our hearts to your will. We give you all the praise in the Holy Name of Jesus. Amen.

INTRODUCTION:

After much Biblical research, I have concluded there were seven covenants that God made with man (see Appendix D); although some scholars claim there were eight covenants. As shown in the referenced Appendix, some covenants were conditional, meaning that man had a requirement or commitment. Some covenants were unconditional, meaning that God made a promise or commitment to man with no strings attached. Most times, when God made a covenant with mankind, it often began a new dispensation of time (see Appendix C). With the fall of Adam and Eve, the Dispensation of Innocence ended, and the Dispensation of Conscience began.

It is important for Christians to study and understand the Abrahamic Covenant. This covenant began a new dispensation of time. The coming of the Messiah was promised in God's covenant with Abraham, and Jesus was a descendant of Abraham.

Abraham is sometimes referred to as "Father Abraham." It could be said that this great man is a type and shadow of God our Father. I am not suggesting that Abraham was divine in any way; indeed, Abraham was a man who occasionally sinned. However, Abraham was the only man in the Bible whom God required to sacrifice his only begotten son. In doing so, God was testing

Abraham's faith in Him. The example of how God would someday offer His only begotten Son as a sacrifice for the sins of mankind was established.

Three religions, still in practice today, have their roots back to Abraham:

- Christianity
- Judaism
- Islam

Because it's everlasting, the Abrahamic covenant remains in effect. Therefore, the Abrahamic covenant has implications for us today, almost 4,000 years later. In this study, we will explore the significance of this covenant to those in our era.

There were ten generations between Noah and Abraham. Abraham lived to be 175 years old.

STUDY:

Read Genesis 17:1-5

How old was Abram when God made His covenant with him?

What new name did God give Abram?

Read Genesis 17:6-8

Describe the seven key promises in the Abrahamic covenant.

Is the covenant that God made with Abraham still in effect today?

It is amazing to consider that God would approach Abram at 99 years of age to make His covenant with him. I wonder how Abram must have felt for God Almighty to appear to him and command that he walk before God and be blameless. Keep in mind that the Law did not exist then. Neither was there a Bible for Abram to follow. Abram could only rely on his sense of right and wrong to guide his actions and live a blameless life before God.

In Genesis 17:5, it says that God gave Abram the new name "Abraham."

- Abram: Great Father, or Father of height
- Abraham: Father of a multitude

In Genesis 17:7, we learn that the Abrahamic covenant would be everlasting. Therefore, the covenant is still in effect today and applies to us living in the 21st century.

There are several key aspects of the Abrahamic covenant:

1. God will multiply Abraham exceedingly (verse 2).
2. Abraham will be the Father of many nations (verse 4).
3. Abraham will be exceedingly fruitful (verse 6).
4. Kings will come from Abraham's seed (verse 6).
5. God will establish His covenant with Abraham *and* with his seed (verse 7).
6. God will be a God unto Abraham *and* to his seed (verse 7).
7. God will give Abraham and his seed the land of Canaan for an everlasting possession (verse 8).

Regarding point number six, above, God will be the God of Abraham and his descendants. Thus, the descendants of Abraham are the *people of God*. Some theologians refer to them as the *children of God*.

Read Genesis 17:9-14
What did God require Abraham to do as a token of the covenant?

What was the fate of a man without circumcision?

What did it mean for a man to be "cut off" from his people?

Why did God choose to require Abraham and his male descendants to be circumcised as a token of the covenant? The answer to this question will become clearer as you progress through this study. Until then, consider that circumcision is the *cutting away of flesh*. Further, circumcision results in the shedding of blood. Recall our previous studies, the punishment for sin is death through the shedding of blood. Although circumcision is not a complete death, it aligns with the punishment for sin.

Notice in Genesis 17:14, a man who was not circumcised was cut off from his people. That may seem harsh, but consider the consequences of this non-action. Essentially, the person was refusing to accept God's covenant. In failing to be circumcised, he was no longer a child of God. He was no longer in a covenant relationship with the God of Abraham.

Fill in the blanks for this key passage:

GALATIANS 6:16 (KJV)

And as _____ as walk according to this rule, peace be on them, and mercy, and upon the _____ of _____ .

The phrase "Israel of God" is only used one time in the Bible, in Galatians 6:16. Some believe this phrase is describing the Jews (descendants of Abraham) who had also obeyed the Gospel and received the Holy Spirit (see Acts, Chapter 2). This phrase describes *all* who received the Holy Spirit, both Jews and Gentiles.

Regardless, my research into this phrase led me full circle back to the Abrahamic covenant. It confirmed that with this covenant, there is the *God* of the covenant, and the *Man* (Israel) of the covenant. The conclusion being that the people included in the Abrahamic covenant are indeed the chosen people of God, and the children of God (e.g., the Israel of God).

Now, let's turn our attention to the New Testament and explore the implications of the Abrahamic covenant to people today.

Fill in the blanks for this key passage:

COLOSSIANS 2:10-12 (KJV)

And ye are complete in him, which is the head of all principality and power: In whom also ye are _____with the circumcision made without hands, in the putting of the body of the _____ _____ _____ _____ by the circumcision of Christ: _____ with him in _____, wherein also ye are risen with him through the faith of the operation of God, who hath raised him from the dead.

How is circumcision in the Old Testament symbolic of repentance for us today?

What is accomplished with the circumcision made without hands?

How are we "buried" with Christ?

It is interesting to see the choice of words Paul uses in Colossians chapter two to describe the repentance process. He relates to his audience, who were familiar with the concept of circumcision as a token of the Abrahamic covenant. Paul is confirming that circumcision is still required. Not the physical circumcision, but the spiritual circumcision of the heart by Christ. Putting off the carnal, sinful nature through the repentance process.

Paul once again confirmed the necessity of baptism in Colossians 2:12. We must be buried with Jesus, not physically, but spiritually, by being symbolically buried with Jesus in water baptism. Since Jesus is the one who died and was buried, it is important to call His name during baptism. We will explore this further in an upcoming study.

Fill in the blanks for this key passage:

ROMANS 2:28-29 (KJV)

For he is not a _____, which is one outwardly; neither is that _____, which is outward in the flesh: But he is a _____, which is one inwardly; and circumcision is that of the _____, in the _____, and not in the letter; whose praise is not of men, but of God.

What do these two scriptures mean to you?

_____

_____

_____

Is physical circumcision still required today for salvation?

_____

_____

_____

Being a descendant of Abraham and practicing the law of circumcision and atonement would no longer secure their salvation. What a shock for the Jews of the first century to learn this. Personally, I can understand how many of the Jews in that era had difficulty accepting Christ. Imagine being a child of God one day, then a few days later, you are told that you are no longer a child of God. Accepting Christ and obeying His Gospel are now required for salvation (see Romans 9:8).

However, history confirms that many Jews obeyed the Gospel of Jesus Christ and received the gift of the Holy Spirit. Many of these new converts, unfortunately, held on to the law or some aspects of the law. Later, when the Holy Spirit was poured out on the Gentiles, some of the Jewish converts insisted that the Gentiles needed to be circumcised under the Abrahamic covenant. In much of Paul's writing, he was battling this false doctrine and reassuring the Gentiles that physical circumcision was no longer required.

Paul was bold enough to declare in Romans 9:8 that the physical descendants of Abraham are *no longer* the children of God. Instead, the children of the promise (those filled with the Holy Spirit) are counted for the seed (descendants of Abraham).

The question regarding the need to be circumcised was so prevalent among the early church that a special council in Jerusalem addressed the issue in Acts, Chapter 15. In this account, both Peter and Paul argued that those Gentiles receiving the Holy Spirit did not need to be burdened any further with the practice of circumcision, which was required under the Abrahamic covenant. The council consented to this logic and wrote a letter to the Gentiles, which documented their decision (see Acts 15:28).

Let us turn our attention back to the book of Genesis and explore the Abrahamic covenant in more detail. The following text follows the account where God asked Abraham to sacrifice his only begotten son, Isaac. If you are not familiar with this account, I suggest you read Genesis 22:1-14.

Some theologians believe that the mount on which Abraham attempted to offer Isaac as a sacrifice is the same mount where Jesus Christ was later crucified. However, this cannot be substantiated in the Bible. Abraham's willingness to sacrifice Isaac was a type and shadow of our Heavenly Father offering His only begotten Son, Jesus, for a sacrifice.

Read Genesis 22:15-18

What were two analogies God used to tell Abraham that He would multiply his seed?

What is the significance of the analogies to stars and sand?

What did God promise Abraham's seed to possess?

Who would be blessed by Abraham's seed?

In verse 17 of the above text, we read how God promised to multiply Abraham's seed:

- As the *stars* of the Heaven,
- As the *sand* on the seashore. [Emphasis added]

We cannot count the number of stars in the Heavens, nor can we count the grains of sand on the seashore. These two references are not to be taken literally. Rather, Abraham's descendants would be many and far too many to count. Notice the two references; one being *sand,* which is symbolic of the physical, biological descendants of Abraham. Whenever we consider stars, we envision Heavenly objects. Therefore, the reference to *stars* relates to the *spiritual* descendants of Abraham.

The reference to *Abraham's seed* (singular) in verses 17 and 18 of Genesis 22 is a direct reference to Jesus Christ. We discovered in our study of the fall of Adam and Eve, the first Messianic prophecy of Christ *crushing* the head of Satan. In Genesis, Chapter 22, this is expanded to state that the Messiah would possess the gate of His enemy. Further, we read that all the nations would be blessed; this refers to the gift of salvation through the sacrifice of Christ.

Fill in the blanks for this key passage:

GALATIANS 3:27-29 (KJV)

For as many of you as have been _____ into Christ have put on Christ. There is neither _____ nor _____, there is neither bond nor free, there is neither male nor female: for ye are all one in _____ _____. And if ye be _____, then are ye _____ seed and _____ according to the promise.

Who do we "put on" whenever we are baptized into Christ?

If we are Christ's, whose seed are we from (spiritually)?

In John 3:1-8, we find the recorded conversation between Jesus and a Pharisee by the name of Nicodemus. In verse five of this text, Jesus advised Nicodemus that a man must be born of the water and of the Spirit to enter the kingdom of God. Nicodemus was initially confused by Jesus' reference to being *born again*. However, Jesus explained further in verse six of this text that He was speaking of a *spiritual* birth.

In our earlier study of the fall of man, we established that our spirits are dead because of sin. Further, we established that all have sinned and therefore all of humanity is dead in spirit. Thanks be to God that believers today can experience this *new birth* experience with the gift of the Holy Spirit that Jesus described to Nicodemus.

Whenever a person experiences spiritual rebirth by receiving the Holy Spirit, they must have a birthing father. Who is the Father? *Jesus Christ* is the *Father*, as Paul explained in Galatians 3:27-29. Jesus is our spiritual Father and a descendant of Abraham. Those who receive the gift of the Holy Spirit become spiritual descendants of Abraham. They are, therefore, under the Abrahamic covenant. Those experiencing the spiritual new birth become one of the *stars* that God references in Genesis, Chapter 22.

CONCLUSION:

The study of the Abrahamic covenant is rich in spiritual significance that spans much of the Bible. We established that Abraham's descendants would be the people of God (the Israel of God). We also established that the Abrahamic covenant is everlasting and therefore still in effect today. With this covenant, a new dispensation of time began; the Dispensation of Promise (see Appendix C).

What was the promise that God made to Abraham? There were several aspects of the promise:

- Many descendants were promised, and many nations and kings.
- Abraham and his descendants were promised fruitfulness and blessings.
- The land of Canaan was promised to Abraham's descendants as an everlasting possession.
- Both biological and spiritual descendants were promised to Abraham.

The promise also included the prophecy of the Messiah, who would be Abraham's seed (see Galatians 3:16). The Messiah would possess the gates of His enemy. Jesus' sacrifice at Calvary would bless all nations.

Logic suggests that one must be a descendant of Abraham and heir to the promises of the Abrahamic covenant to be *a child of God*. Before the outpouring of the Holy Spirit in Acts, Chapter 2, Abraham's biological descendants were indeed the children of God, provided they obeyed the requirements of circumcision and later followed the Law and the rituals of atonement. These descendants may be thought of as *sand* (biological descendants of Abraham) in relation to the Abrahamic covenant. However, this dynamic changed altogether with the outpouring of the Holy

Spirit in Acts 2. Starting then, only the spiritual descendants of Christ and Abraham were counted as children of God. Those who receive the gift of the Holy Spirit become children of God. According to the Abrahamic covenant, these spiritual descendants are referred to as *stars*.

For us today, whenever a person receives the Holy Spirit and is baptized with Christ, they experience the *new birth* that Jesus explained to Nicodemus in John chapter 3. With the new birth, the dead spirit within a person is resurrected and becomes alive, thus the term *new birth*. I am convinced that Jesus Christ is a proud Father with each spiritual birth that occurs.

In this study, we learned that circumcision was required in the Old Testament as a token of the Abrahamic covenant. The act of circumcision was symbolic of repentance for us today. Whenever we repent and turn from our sins, and crucify our carnal flesh (sinful nature), our sins are forgiven (atoned by the blood of Jesus). And Christ performs a circumcision of our hearts, cutting away the sinful nature. Ezekiel prophesied in Chapter 36, verses 26-27, that God would give us a new heart and a new spirit. God would also take away the heart of stone and replace it with a heart of flesh. This prophecy is fulfilled each time a person experiences the gift of the Holy Spirit.

SELF-REFLECTION:

Describe the key points you learned from the study of the Abrahamic covenant.

In what ways can you implement these key points for a better relationship with God?

STUDY NINE: *Feast of Passover*

OPENING PRAYER:

Heavenly Father, thank you for sending your son as the perfect and spotless lamb of God. As we open your Word and study the Feast of Passover, give each of us a new appreciation for how great and perfect you are. Prepare our minds and our hearts to receive and obey your Word. May we be strengthened and blessed as we submit our hearts to your will. We give you all the praise in the Holy Name of Jesus. Amen.

INTRODUCTION:

One of my favorite Bible studies is the account of the Passover. It was the final Egyptian plague of the Death Angel that ultimately convinced Pharaoh to release the Israelites from slavery. Although the history leading up to this event is not within the scope of this book, I will provide a summary below of the history leading up to the Israelites' slavery by the Egyptians. If you are not familiar with this history, I suggest that you take the time to read this fascinating account in Genesis, Chapters 37 through 50.

In our study of the Abrahamic Covenant, I touched on the fact that Abraham had a son (Isaac) by his wife, Sarah. Abraham had two grandsons, Esau and Jacob, through Isaac. Then Jacob, who had the birthright, had 12 sons. Jacob's name was changed to Israel during his encounter with God (see Genesis 32:24-32). These 12 men became the original tribes of Israel; however, the names of the 12 tribes of Israel changed over time (see Appendix F for details).

Joseph, who was a dreamer, was Jacob's favorite son, which caused his brothers to hate him. His brothers plotted against him and sold him into slavery. After many unfortunate events as a slave and prisoner in Egypt, Joseph found favor with Pharaoh. He had interpreted two prophetic dreams that Pharaoh had dreamed. These dreams foretold a great famine. Joseph was then promoted to Ruler of Egypt and charged with collecting and storing food stock to prepare for the famine.

Just as Joseph had interpreted Pharaoh's dreams, the famine occurred, which affected the entire region. He was reunited with his father, Jacob (Israel), and his brothers and their families when they sought food in Egypt during the famine. Historians have estimated that their move to Egypt occurred around 1876 BC. The Israelites (Jews) remained in Egypt after the famine and prospered under Joseph's fame and influence.

Unfortunately, after Joseph expired, a new Pharaoh rose to power who did not know Joseph. He viewed the Israelites living in Egypt as a threat and enslaved them. According to historical recordings, the Israelites lived in Egypt for 430 years, of which 400 years were spent in slavery to the Egyptians. (see Acts 7:6 and Genesis 15:13) Some historians speculate that the Israelite slaves labored to build the great cities of Egypt, primarily making the building materials by hand.

As slavery became more unbearable, the Israelites called out to God, and He heard their cries. Remembering His covenant with Abraham, God raised Moses and his brother Aaron to lead His people (the Israelites) from Egyptian slavery. By the hand of Moses, God wrought ten plagues upon Pharaoh and the Egyptians. Each of these plagues represented God's wrath and curse against the false gods of Egypt. For those interested in learning more, see Appendix G for details.

The last of these plagues, the tenth, was the Death Angel passing over the land of Egypt, slaying the firstborn of both man and beast. However, the Israelites were protected against God's wrath by sacrificing an animal and applying its blood on their doorposts and side posts; this was a type of atonement.

During this study, we will establish the symbolic meaning of the sacrificial animal and how it relates to the death of Jesus Christ in the New Testament. Several historical concepts are key to fully understanding Passover. For example, before we begin this study, here is some helpful information on relating dates and times in the Old and New Testaments.

First, one must understand the way time was measured by the Jewish people back in the Old Testament era. According to the Jewish (Hebrew) Day, a day ended at sundown (12th hour of the day), which is approximately 6 p.m. on our time scale. Essentially, their day began six hours ahead of our modern Day (See Appendix E). There were four watches of the night, three hours each. Then, as day broke, the sundial was used to track the hours of the day. For example, the third hour of the day was 9 a.m. (our time), the sixth hour of the day was noon, and the ninth hour of the day was 3 p.m., etc.

Exodus 12:6 is a key passage in understanding when the Israelites sacrificed lambs during Passover, according to the Old Testament. Examining the actual Hebrew text provides clarity on the timing for this event. In the KJV translation, this scripture reads: And ye shall keep it up until the fourteenth day of the same month: and the whole assembly of the congregation of Israel shall kill it in the evening. "In the evening" in the original Hebrew text is *beyn ha-arbayim*. This Hebrew term means "between two evenings."

As you will see from the Hebrew Day in Appendix E, the *first evening* begins whenever the sun crests, which is the sixth hour of the day, and ends at the ninth hour of the day. The *second evening*, then, is from the ninth hour of the day until the 12th hour of the day.

Therefore, we can conclude that *between the two evenings* is the ninth hour of the day. On today's clock, this equates to 3 p.m.

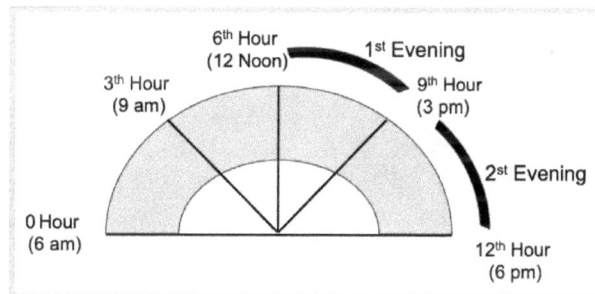

STUDY:

God ordained the Feast of Passover (Pesach in Hebrew) to commemorate the last (tenth) plague in Egypt, which ultimately resulted in the freeing of the Israelites from 400 years of slavery. The Feast of Passover was one of the seven God ordained convocations. Refer to Appendix A and Appendix B for details regarding the seven Old Testament convocations. Details of these convocations are recorded in chapter 23 of Leviticus. Note that the first month on the Jewish calendar is Nisan (Abib in Hebrew), which begins mid-March on the Gregorian calendar.

Read Exodus 12:1-5

What month and day did God instruct the Israelites to take a lamb into their home?

Describe the criteria for selecting the lamb?

In what ways does the lamb in this text relate to Jesus Christ?

God instructed the Israelites to select their sacrificial lamb on the 10th of Nisan, which is the first month on the Jewish calendar. According to Jewish history, the lamb was to be kept in their homes, to be cared for and tested to ensure there were no blemishes. Some theologians interpret the text regarding the *male of the first year* to mean the firstborn male of the mother sheep or goat (firstborn son). This would certainly lend more specificity to the lamb being symbolic of the Messiah. In either case, the symbolism remains that the male lamb, without blemish, is a type and shadow of the future Lamb of God. Jesus was a male without blemish (sin).

In verse five of this text, we read that the lamb must be a male of the first year and could be taken from the sheep or the goats. The fact that both sheep and goats were allowed as a sacrifice has spiritual significance. Jesus uses the analogy in Matthew chapter 25 of sheep and goats. Sheep are the born-again believers; goats are non-believers. But yet, both sheep and goats were allowed as sacrificial lambs. Let's explore the reason. Fill in the blanks for these key passages:

MATTHEW 25:32-34, 41 (NIV)

All the nations will be gathered before Him, and He will separate the people one from another as a shepherd separates the _____ from the _____. He will put the _____ on His _____ and the _____ on His _____. Then the King will say to those on His _____, "Come you who are blessed by my Father; take your inheritance, the kingdom prepared for you since the creation of the world." Then He will say to those on His _____, "Depart from me, you who are cursed, into the eternal fire prepared for the devil and his angels."

In this reading, we see where God uses the analogy that sheep are saved Christians and goats are non-believers. Yet both are acceptable as sacrificial animals in the book of Exodus. To fully understand the rationale, consider the genealogy of Jesus Christ. Although most of Christ's bloodline was Jewish, there were several Gentile women in the genealogy of Jesus. Those women were Tamar, Rahab, Ruth, and Bathsheba. NOTE: If you are not familiar with this genealogy, read Matthew 1:1-17 for details. Therefore, it is logical that both sheep and goat sacrifices would represent the symbolic type and shadow of the future Messiah, since Jesus had both Jews and Gentiles in His bloodline.

Fill in the blanks for these key passages:

EXODUS 12:6 (KJV)

And ye shall _____ it up until the _____ day of the same month (Nisan): and the whole assembly of the congregation of Israel shall _____ it in the evening.

Reference the introduction of this study and review the meaning of *in the evening* in the Hebrew text. What day and time of day were the Israelites instructed to slay their lambs?

_____th day of Nisan   _____th hour of the day

It is important to understand that the sacrificial lambs were slain at the 9th hour of the day (between the two evenings) in the account of the Exodus Passover. Later in this study, we will establish how this timing relates to the death of Jesus Christ on the cross.

Read Exodus 12:7-11

How does applying the blood of the lamb on the doorposts relate to our salvation?

What were they expected to do with the slain lamb?

What was this event called?

We learned in these scriptures that the sacrificial lambs were slain at the ninth hour of the day on the 14th of Nisan. The Israelites were instructed to apply the blood to the doorposts of their homes. Recall our study of Atonement. The blood of the lamb on their doorposts would atone their homes from the wrath of God whenever the death angel passed over the land. This is spiritually symbolic to us today in that we must apply the blood of Jesus to the *doorposts of our hearts* to atone for our sins.

Further, we learned that the slain lambs were to be roasted with bitter herbs, then consumed with unleavened bread (bread without yeast). We read in Exodus 12:11 that this event is called the *Lord's Passover*. However, the Death Angel passed over the land of Egypt, slaying all the firstborn at midnight, which would have been the next day (15th of Nisan). See Exodus 12:29 for details. As we progress in this study, it is important to understand the difference between the Lord's Passover and Passover (reference Appendix A).

Nisan 14th	Lord's Passover	Lamb slain at the 9th hour of the day
Nisan 15th	Passover	Death Angel passes over Egypt

Fill in the blanks for this key passage:

JOHN 6:53-54 (NIV)

Jesus said unto them, "Very truly I tell you, unless you _____ the _____ of the Son of Man and _____ His _____, you have no life in you. Whoever eats my _____ and drinks my _____ has eternal life, and I will raise them up at the last day."

Contrast the consumption of the lamb in Exodus to the consumption of the Body of Christ described in John 6:

_____

_____

_____

_____

_____

In Jesus' day, many of His followers left Him after the statements He made, which are recorded in John 6:53-54. These words must have been repulsive to those listening that day. Obviously, they did not understand that He was referring to a spiritual consumption of His body and blood. Whenever we contrast the lamb in Exodus to Christ, we see that the lamb in Exodus was a type and shadow of the Lamb of God. While the lamb in Exodus was consumed literally, the body of Christ must be consumed spiritually for salvation. The lamb in Exodus was roasted with bitter herbs, whereas the crucifixion of Christ was indeed a bitter death.

Notice that the bread in the Exodus text was required to be unleavened. As most bakers know, leaven (yeast) is a contaminant. It decomposes the fine flour, which causes the dough to rise as the decomposition gases are released. But what is the spiritual significance of the unleavened bread? Leaven (or yeast) is symbolic of sin, which decomposes the flour. The fine flour represents the perfect and sinless body of Christ. In Acts 2:27b, the Bible states that "Thine Holy One will not see corruption."

The following table compares the unleavened bread in Exodus to Christ:

UNLEAVENED BREAD	JESUS CHRIST
Fine Flour	Body of Christ
Without Leaven	Without Sin

Read Exodus 12:12-15

Describe the judgment that God promised to execute against Egypt.

How were the houses of the Israelites protected from this last plague?

How many days were they instructed to eat unleavened bread?

According to verse 15, what would happen to a person who did not follow the instructions and ate leavened bread?

The punishment of being "cut off" from Israel seems extreme. Why did God choose this punishment?

As we have read, the tenth and last plague in Egypt was the Passover of the Lord (as the Death Angel), where every firstborn of man and beast would be slain. This last plague was a direct curse against Pharaoh (see Appendix G for details), who claimed to be the son of Ra, the Sun God. Since Pharaoh claimed to be the son of a god, the God of Israel destroyed Pharaoh's son, along with all the firstborn across Egypt.

In Exodus 12, the Israelites were protected (atoned) from the wrath of God by the blood of their sacrificial lambs on their doorposts. Today, the blood of Jesus Christ must be applied to our lives spiritually to gain salvation. We will cover this in more detail later in this book.

It has also been established that yeast is symbolic of sin because it is a contaminant that decomposes the fine flour. Since the fine flour represented the sinless body of Christ, the Israelites were forbidden to eat leavened bread for seven days. Historians believe that the Egyptian armies were finally destroyed at the crossing of the Red Sea seven days after the Israelites left Egypt.

Many believe that the requirement to avoid leavened bread for seven days coincided with the timing of the Israelites' freedom from Egyptian slavery. For those not familiar with this event, I would recommend that you read Exodus, Chapter 14.

Since the unleavened bread is a type and shadow of the sinless body of Christ, anyone who ate leavened bread during these seven days, as described in the Exodus text, was *cut off* from their people. Our study of the Abrahamic covenant showed us that people who were *cut off* were no longer in the covenant. Therefore, they were no longer considered children of God.

It may seem like an extreme punishment; however, consider the implications of consuming leavened bread. The individual eating leavened bread was proclaiming that the coming Messiah would *not* have a sinless life! By doing so, they were rejecting the Messiah and His ability to save His people.

Next, let's turn our attention to the New Testament and connect the Old Testament account of the Passover to Christ.

Fill in the blanks for this key passage:

JOHN 1:29 (NIV)

The next day, John saw Jesus coming toward him and said, "Look, the _____ of _____, who takes away the sin of the world!"

Imagine being a Jew in AD 30, listening to John the Baptist make this declaration. Now that you better understand the Passover feast, what thoughts would you have?

_____

_____

_____

_____

Keep in mind that the Jews celebrated the Feast of Passover year after year, and they would have been accustomed to selecting their sacrificial lamb on the 10th of Nisan. I can envision the fathers, including their sons, selecting their lamb and inspecting it to ensure there were no blemishes. Then on the 14th of Nisan, they would slay the lamb during the 9th hour of the day and roast it along with bitter herbs. I can only imagine the feast, which also included unleavened bread, and the celebration that took place while they reflected on God's delivery of their ancestors from Egyptian slavery.

The Israelites clearly understood the significance of the sacrificial lamb that was slain, which ultimately resulted in their freedom from slavery. Then, they heard John the Baptist announce that this man named Jesus was the *Lamb of God* sent to take away the sin of the world. I'm sure that some of John's audience understood this connection. Unfortunately, many completely missed the connection altogether. To set the stage for the next part of the study, we will concentrate on the week of Jesus' crucifixion.

Fill in the blanks for this key passage:

JOHN 12:1 (NIV)

_____ days before Passover, Jesus arrived in Bethany, where Lazarus lived, whom Jesus had raised from the dead.

Note: the Passover in this scripture is in reference to the day the Death Angel passed over the land of Egypt (Nisan 15th).

What day of Nisan did Jesus travel to Bethany? (Hint: 15-6)?

JOHN 12:12-13 (NIV)

The _____ day the great crowd that had come for the Feast heard that Jesus was on His way to Jerusalem. They took _____ branches and went out to meet him, shouting, "Hosanna! Blessed is He who comes in the name of the Lord! Blessed is the King of Israel!"

The text above describes Jesus' triumphal entry into Jerusalem, which occurred only a few days before His crucifixion.

What date in Nisan was Jesus' triumphal entry into Jerusalem? (Hint: 9 + 1 = _____)

How does the date (day of month) of Jesus' Triumphal Entry compare to the selection of the sacrificial lambs in Exodus?

It is so amazing that our God knew the exact day that Jesus would ride into Jerusalem, the House of Israel, before His death. God then strategically planned the events in Exodus to coincide perfectly with the events that would occur 1,478 years later. Back in Egypt, at the time of the Passover, God gave the Israelites specific instructions to select their sacrificial lambs on the 10th day of Nisan. God knew that on the anniversary of this day, Jesus, the selected Lamb of God, would likewise make His Triumphal Entry into Jerusalem, the House of Israel.

Nisan 10th, 1446 BC	The Passover Lamb is selected and brought into the home.
Nisan 10th, AD 33	Jesus Christ's Triumphal Entry into Jerusalem.

Now we will explore the last few hours before Jesus was crucified.
Fill in the blanks for this key passage:

LUKE 22:7-8 (NIV)
Then came the day of the Unleavened Bread on which the Passover _____
had to be sacrificed. Jesus sent Peter and John, saying, "Go and make preparations for us to eat
the _____."

In this text, Jesus and His disciples are planning their preparations for the Last Supper. Notice that the day on which the Passover lamb was to be slain has started. Remember, the Hebrew day began at 6 p.m.

Read Luke 22:9-20

What day of Nisan (the first month on the Hebrew calendar) did the Last Supper occur?

What did Jesus proclaim that He would *not* consume until the kingdom of God was fulfilled?

Describe what the unleavened bread and wine represented at the Last Supper:

As we learned earlier in this study, the date on which the Passover lamb was slain first began back in Egypt (Exodus 12) was Nisan 14th (The Lord's Passover). Then, 1,478 years later, Jesus hosted the Last Supper on the anniversary of the Lord's Passover.

At the Last Supper, Jesus proclaims He will not eat or drink of a Passover meal again until the kingdom of God has come. He further explained that the unleavened bread represented His sinless body, and the wine represented His blood, which would be shed for them.

Perhaps you are not familiar with the events that occurred on this same day (after the Last Supper), which led to Jesus' arrest, mock trial, crucifixion, and burial. If so, I recommend the following scriptures for your reference:

EVENT	Matthew	Mark	Luke	John
Last Supper	26:17-29	14:12-25	22:7-25	13:1-38
Garden of Gethsemane	26:36-46	14:32-42	22:40-46	18:1
Jesus' Arrest	26:47-75	14:43-72	22:47-71	18:2-28
Mock Trial	27:1-26	15:1-15	23:1-25	18:29—19:16
Crucifixion	27:27-56	15:16-41	23:26-49	19:17-30
Burial	27:57-66	15:42-47	23:50-56	19:31-42

Fill in the blanks for this key passage:

JOHN 19:4 (KJV)

Pilate therefore went forth again, and saith unto them, Behold, I bring Him forth to you, that ye may know that I find _____ _____ in Him.

What was the significance of Pilate's declaration that there was "no fault" in Jesus?

_____

_____

_____

Pilate had to confront a volatile situation. He kept peace and order in his area of jurisdiction. If the Jewish religious leaders did not get their way and have Jesus crucified, then the emperor of Rome would certainly hear about it. Pilate would then lose his prestige (or perhaps even worse). However, he knew Jesus was, in fact, innocent, and he had a moral responsibility to render judgment according to his conscience. In the end, he yielded to the political pressure over his conscience and allowed the Jews to win.

It is unlikely that Pilate knew how prophetic his declaration was that day when he declared that Jesus Christ was without fault. Just as the Israelites inspected their lambs back in Egypt to ensure their sacrifices were without blemish (faultless), likewise, Jesus was inspected and declared to be without blemish or faultless.

The population of the Israelites leaving Egypt was 600,000 men, not including children.

You'll find a timeline below that details the events around Jesus' arrest, trial, crucifixion, and burial, according to the texts as mentioned earlier.

Contrast the date and time that the sacrificial lambs were slain in Egypt with the date and time that Jesus died on the cross:

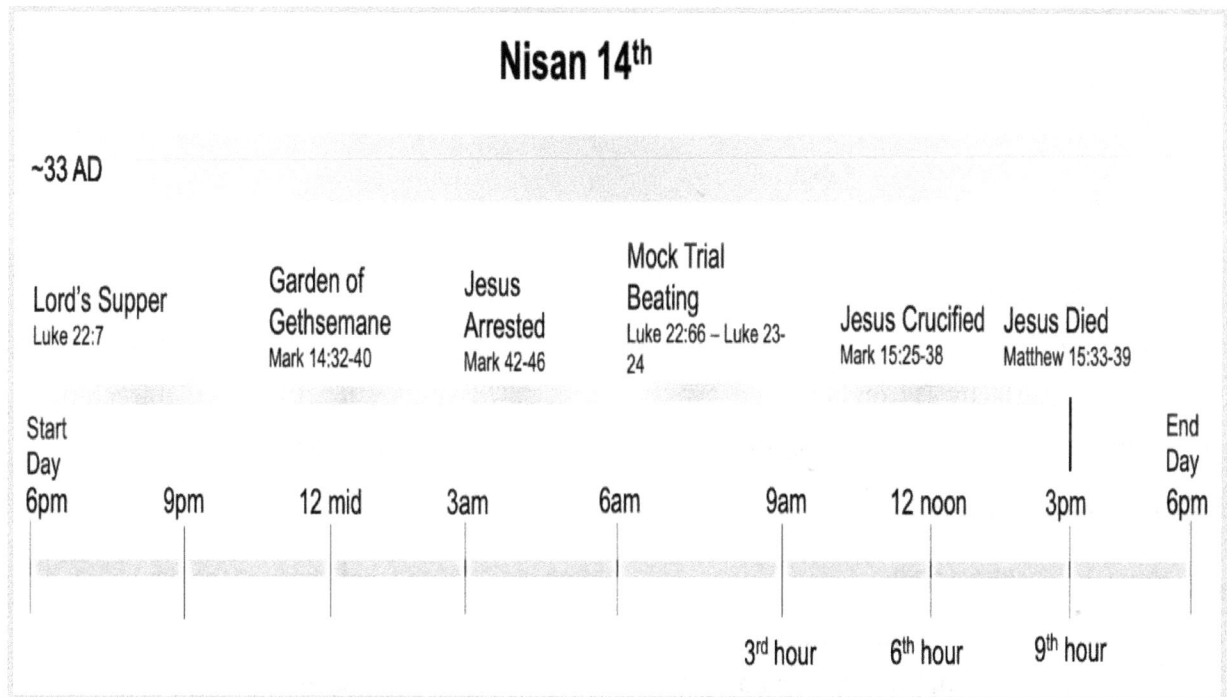

Nisan 14th

~33 AD

| Lord's Supper
Luke 22:7 | Garden of Gethsemane
Mark 14:32-40 | Jesus Arrested
Mark 42-46 | Mock Trial Beating
Luke 22:66 – Luke 23-24 | Jesus Crucified
Mark 15:25-38 | Jesus Died
Matthew 15:33-39 |

Start Day 6pm	9pm	12 mid	3am	6am	9am	12 noon	3pm	End Day 6pm
					3rd hour	6th hour	9th hour	

You might have observed how descriptive and precise God's instructions to the Israelites were in the narrative of the Passover plague. This study highlights why their instructions were so exact. Their actions were foreshadowing events that would happen in the distant future by mirroring the Messiah's last days before His death.

The outline below illustrates the event in Egypt and shows how it aligns with Jesus.

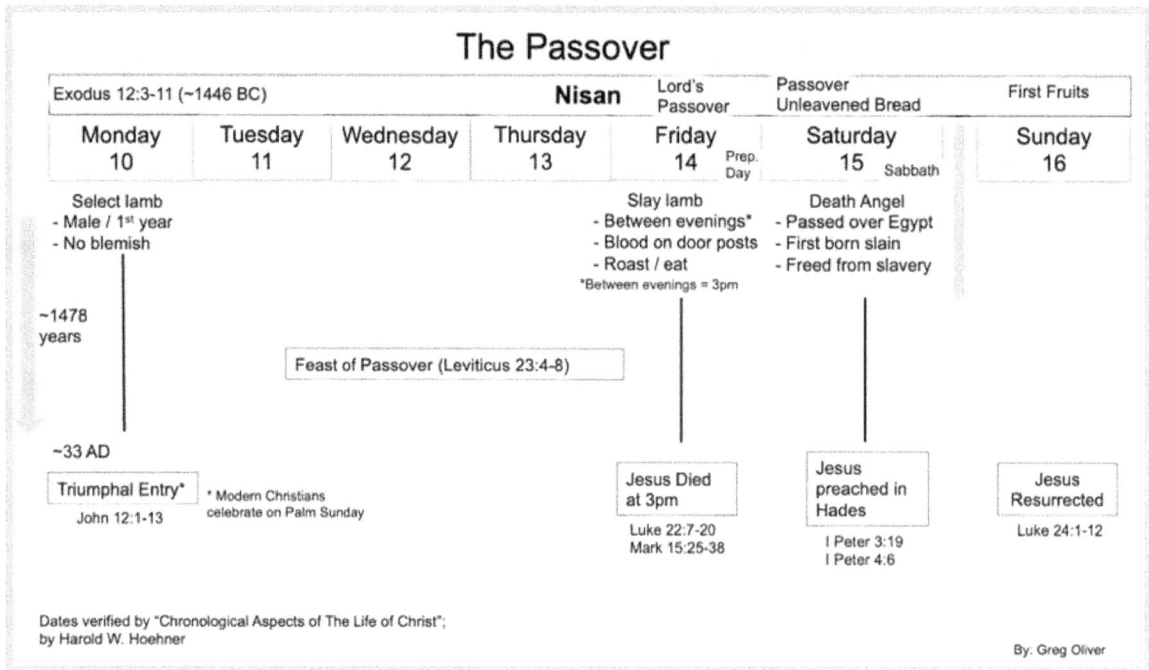

The Passover

Exodus 12:3-11 (~1446 BC)			**Nisan**	Lord's Passover	Passover Unleavened Bread	First Fruits
Monday 10	Tuesday 11	Wednesday 12	Thursday 13	Friday 14 Prep. Day	Saturday 15 Sabbath	Sunday 16

Select lamb
- Male / 1st year
- No blemish

Slay lamb
- Between evenings*
- Blood on door posts
- Roast / eat
*Between evenings = 3pm

Death Angel
- Passed over Egypt
- First born slain
- Freed from slavery

~1478 years

Feast of Passover (Leviticus 23:4-8)

~33 AD

Triumphal Entry*
John 12:1-13
* Modern Christians celebrate on Palm Sunday

Jesus Died at 3pm
Luke 22:7-20
Mark 15:25-38

Jesus preached in Hades
I Peter 3:19
I Peter 4:6

Jesus Resurrected
Luke 24:1-12

Dates verified by "Chronological Aspects of The Life of Christ"; by Harold W. Hoehner

By: Greg Oliver

CONCLUSION:

Our God is perfect in all of His ways. In the study of the Passover and how it relates to Christ Jesus, we see how perfectly He orchestrated events across 1,478 years, such that they miraculously correlate. Not only do the dates align, but also the exact timing as well. In summary:

NISAN 10TH	NISAN 14TH (At the ninth hour of the day)
Israelites brought a lamb into their homes	Israelites slayed a sacrificial lamb
Jesus' Triumphal Entry into Jerusalem	Jesus died on the cross

Comparing these two events, we see how the first Lord's Passover brought freedom from *physical* slavery, whereas the sacrifice of Jesus brought freedom from *spiritual* slavery. Perhaps it was God's will all along for the Israelites to suffer and endure slavery so that He could prove His awesome power to them while also giving them an example of redemption. By having this example, surely, they should have been able to recognize the Messiah whenever He arrived on the scene to rescue them from spiritual slavery. After all, they understood the significance of the *sacrificial lamb*, which brought them out of Egypt.

The more we study the Bible, the more it becomes clear that our God hates idolatry. Yet man, whom He created, worshipped other facets of His Creation. How insulting that must have been to God. And to add insult to injury, Pharaoh dared to claim to be a son of Ra, the Sun God.

God's plan was brilliant! He would show His almighty power to His people while simultaneously destroying the mighty empire of Egypt, which worshipped idols and self-elevated itself as gods. All while giving His people an unforgettable example of freedom for their future reference.

In this study, we established other symbolic comparisons between the Lord's Passover and Christ.

SACRIFICIAL LAMB—UNLEAVENED BREAD	JESUS CHRIST
Lamb—without blemish	Without sin
Lamb—male of the first year	Male—firstborn of God
Lamb—roasted with bitter herbs	Bitter crucifixion
Bread—without leaven	Body—without sin

Today, we celebrate communion with unleavened bread and wine to remember the broken body and blood that Jesus sacrificed to redeem us from spiritual slavery from sin. May this study enrich your spiritual experience every time you take part in a future communion service.

One last comment on Jesus' triumphal entry: Most churches today celebrate this event on Palm Sunday. However, the Triumphal Entry actually occurred on a Monday. For confirmation of this, I refer you to *Chronological Aspects of the Life of Christ* by Harold W. Hoehner.

SELF-REFLECTIONS:

What key point of this study affected you the most?

How has this study affected your perspective on the practice of communion?

Name ways that this study has increased your faith in God:

STUDY TEN: *Redemption from Physical Slavery*

OPENING PRAYER:

Heavenly Father, we thank you for orchestrating the events in the Old Testament to show us your pattern of redemption. I pray that you bring spiritual revelations to each of us as we study the redemption of Israel from Egyptian bondage. We open our minds and hearts to receive your Word. May we be strengthened and blessed as we submit our hearts to your will. We give you all the praise in the Holy Name of Jesus. Amen.

INTRODUCTION:

As a reminder, we established the pattern of redemption in the study on the Gospel of Jesus Christ. The pattern of the good news of the Gospel is:

- Jesus died.
- Jesus was buried.
- Jesus was resurrected from the dead.

In the study of Noah, we discovered the symbolic alignment of Noah and the great flood with the pattern of the Gospel. This was only one of several accounts in the Bible in which this Gospel pattern occurs. Likewise, this same pattern is reflected in the steps that a new believer must take to gain salvation (refer to the study on "Obeying the Gospel of Jesus Christ").

In our previous study on the Lord's Passover, we recognized the correlation between the sacrificial lamb in Exodus and the perfect Lamb of God (Jesus Christ). In this study, we will examine the remaining account of the Israelite's delivery from Egypt, their crossing of the Red Sea, and how the crossing was a typology of baptism. Further, the giving of the Law at Mount Sinai was a type and shadow of resurrection. Following these events, God's plan was for them to inherit the Promised Land, a land flowing with milk and honey. The goal for this study is to uncover the hidden types and shadows of the Gospel pattern: death, burial/baptism, and resurrection.

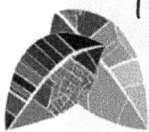

The Pattern of Redemption can be found in various Old Testament accounts.

STUDY:

We have already established the first step in the pattern of the Gospel, which is *death*. As you recall, the Paschal (Passover) lamb was slain on the 14th of Nisan, which aligns perfectly with the first step of the pattern. The first step is the death of Jesus. For the first time in the life of the Israelites who lived on that day in Egypt, they walked out of Egypt on the 15th of Nisan as free men and women. They were liberated at last from their hard bondage. But were they truly free? After all, Pharaoh was still in power in Egypt, and those who had enslaved them were only a short distance away.

Read Exodus 14:5-12
Why did Pharaoh and the Egyptians have a change of heart regarding the release of the Israelites?

What action did Pharaoh take to recapture the Israelites?

How many chariots did Pharaoh assemble to pursue the Israelites?

After enduring 10 plagues, which practically destroyed the land of Egypt, one would think that Pharaoh would have accepted his defeat at the hand of the almighty God of Israel. However, we see in these scriptures that Pharaoh had a change of heart and decided to pursue and recapture his slaves. But why would he make such a foolish decision? Perhaps he realized that he had lost the means to construct his great cities. Now, who would build his edifices? Besides that, he was the son of Ra and a god in his own mind. Ultimately, he had a change of heart because God hardened his heart. God was not through destroying the false god (Pharaoh) permanently.

Pharaoh assembled his army of 600 chariots. Recall from the study of Creation that six is the number for man. I seriously doubt that it is coincidental that Pharaoh used 600 chariots in his conquest. Pharaoh may have believed himself to be a god, but in the end, he was only a man and was no match for the God of the Israelites.

In verse 10 of Exodus 14, we read that the Israelites saw the armies of the Egyptians for the first time since leaving Egypt. They realized that their newly gained freedom was being threatened and maybe even their lives. Imagine the fear that must have rippled through the people as they stood there defenseless against the might of the Egyptian army.

Read Exodus 14:13-20
What encouraging words did Moses speak to the people?

In our lives, how can we use the encouragement Moses gave?

_____

_____

_____

What barrier did God place between the Israelites and the Egyptian army?

_____

_____

_____

In the midst of their greatest fear, the Israelites heard the encouraging words from their leader, Moses, saying, "Don't be afraid, stand still and see the salvation of the Lord." These words are still applicable to our lives today as we face situations that are fearful and even overwhelming. We are blessed to know that our God will fight for us. When we simply do not know what to do or say, our best course of action is to *stand still*, *pray*, and *wait* for God to intervene.

In verse 17, we read that God would take great pleasure in destroying the false god, Pharaoh. Never again would the Israelites need to worry about being slaves to the Egyptians.

Lastly, we read in verses 19-20 where God established a barrier or cloud between the Israelites and their enemies. The enemies were in darkness due to the cloud, whereas the Israelites saw light. From a spiritual perspective, this principle still holds today in that those who obey the Gospel of Jesus Christ live in the light, but the unbelievers live in darkness. (1 Thessalonians 5:5, "Ye are all the children of the light.")

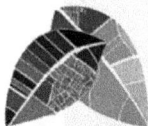

Archeologists claim to have found remnants of Egyptian chariots in the Red Sea.

Read Exodus 14:21-31

Fill in the table below with a summary statement for each verse below and on the next page:

VERSE	KEY ACTION(S):	RESULT(S):
21		
22		
23		
24		
25		
26		
27		
28		

VERSE	KEY ACTION(S):	RESULT(S):
29		
30		
31		

We learn in this reading how God sent a strong *east* wind that parted the Red Sea, allowing the Israelites to pass over the sea on dry land. Throughout the Bible, there is a distinct significance to the directions *East* and *West*. In most cases, moving from east to west is the work of God, or moving towards God, and vice versa, moving toward the east is moving away from God, etc.

Next, we read how the Egyptians pursued the Israelites into the water channel that God had created in the Red Sea. Once there, God caused their chariots' wheels to break apart, thus trapping them. Realizing their dilemma, they attempted to flee from the God of Israel. Then came the grand finale as Moses raised his rod once again, and the waters rushed over the Egyptian forces, completing their destruction. How is the crossing of the Red Sea event relevant to the Gospel of Jesus Christ? Let's explore.

Fill in the blanks of these key passages:

1CORINTHIANS 10:1-4 (KJV)

Moreover, brethren, I would not that ye should be ignorant, how that all our fathers were under the _____, and all passed through the _____; And were all _____ unto Moses in the _____ and in the _____; And did all _____ the same spiritual meat; And did all

THE PATTERN OF REDEMPTION- 119

_____ the same spiritual drink: for they drank of that spiritual Rock that followed them: and that Rock was Christ.

How were the Israelites who left Egypt baptized?

In what way was the Israelites' baptism in the Red Sea symbolic of the Gospel of Jesus Christ?

Do you recall in our study of "Obeying the Gospel of Jesus Christ", we established that water baptism is symbolic of burial? Just as Jesus died and was buried, we must also be buried in baptism with Christ. In like manner, the Israelites, having escaped physical slavery, were then baptized in the Red Sea and further covered in baptism by the cloud.

You may also recall from our previous study that from the time the Israelites walked out of Egypt until the time they were baptized in the Red Sea, they only ate bread without leaven. Their consumption of pure fine flour symbolized the sacrifice of the future Messiah, who knew no sin.

The first Pentecost at Mount Sinai occurred 50 days after the Israelites left Egypt.

Now that we have established how the Israelites' journey to freedom matched two of the steps of the Gospel of Jesus Christ, death and burial/baptism, we will focus on the last element: resurrection. After the crossing of the Red Sea, the Israelites journeyed south until they reached the mountain where Moses had first encountered God at the burning bush. It is here that they received the life-changing Law directly from God Almighty. Let's explore the scriptures to learn more.

Fill in the blanks for the scriptures below:

EXODUS 19:17-20 (NIV)

Then Moses led the people out of the camp to meet with _____, and they stood at the foot of the _____. Mount Sinai was covered with _____, because the Lord descended on it in _____. The smoke billowed up from it like smoke from a furnace, and the whole mountain _____ violently. As the sound of the _____ grew louder and louder., Moses spoke and the voice of _____ answered him. The _____ descended to the top of Mount Sinai and called _____ to the top of the mountain. So Moses went up.

EXODUS 20:1 (NIV)

And _____ spoke all these words...

Recorded in Exodus 20:2-17, God spoke the Ten Commandments to the people. If you are not familiar with the Ten Commandments, I recommend that you familiarize yourself with these commandments.

Describe the scene at Mount Sinai:

_____

_____

_____

How was the giving of the Law at Mount Sinai symbolic of resurrection?

_____

_____

_____

Imagine the fear that swept through the congregation of the Israelites that day as they witnessed firsthand the mighty presence and power of God Almighty descending upon Mount Sinai. The entire mountain must have appeared to be on fire, with smoke and quaking of the surrounding earth. If this was not scary enough, consider hearing the voice of God sounding like the voice of loud trumpets. What an incredible act of God they witnessed.

Later in Exodus chapter 24, we read where God inscribed the Ten Commandments and tablets of stone, which were placed in the Ark of the Covenant. Although it cannot be confirmed in the Bible, Jewish historians have recorded that the giving of the Law on Mount Sinai happened 50 days after the Israelites left Egypt on the day of the first Passover (15th of Nisan). This topic will be covered in more detail in the upcoming study of The Feast of Pentecost.

With the giving of the Law at Mount Sinai, God provided the Israelites a way to deal with their sin issue. Not only did He give them clear guidelines to understand sin, but He also provided the means for atoning for their sins by way of the animal sacrifices. By receiving the Law and agreeing to obey the Law, the Israelites entered a covenant relationship with God. In addition, the nation of Israel experienced a type of resurrection in that they were no longer slaves, but now they were the _Israel of God_ (see Galatians 6:16).

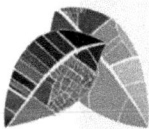

$$Pente = 50$$

Pentecost is the fulfillment of the seven sabbaths:

$$7 \times 7 = 49$$

$$49 + 1 = 50$$

Ten Commandments:

You shall have no other gods before Me.

You shall not make yourself an idol.

You shall not take the name of God in vain.

Remember the sabbath and keep it holy.

Honor your father and your mother.

You shall not murder.

You shall not commit adultery.

You shall not steal.

You shall not give a false testimony.

You shall not covet.

CONCLUSION:

In conclusion, when we step back and consider the account of the Israelites' redemption and delivery from physical slavery, we once again recognize the Redemption pattern. For your convenience, I have expanded the table on the "pattern of the Gospel" to include the account of the Israelites' redemption from Egyptian slavery.

GOSPEL	DEATH	BURIAL	RESURRECTION
Jesus	**Crucified**	**Buried**	**Rose again on the 3rd day**
Believer Obeying the Gospel	**Repents** Dying of Carnal Nature	**Baptized** Buried with Christ Jesus	**Receives the Holy Spirit** Spiritual Birth
Noah and His Family	**Repentance** God repented for creating man	**Burial** Flood buried the Earth	**Resurrection** New life without sin after the Flood
Israelite Slaves Redemption from Slavery	**Death of Paschal Lamb** Means to Freedom, Blood saved them from the wrath of God	**Baptism** Baptized in the Red Sea and the cloud	**Received the Law** Resurrected nation with life-changing Law

With the giving of the Law and Israel's agreement to obey the Law (Exodus 19:8), a new covenant was formed. See Appendix D for details. Along with this new covenant, a new Dispensation of Time also began; the Dispensation of the Law (see Appendix C). This new dispensation of time remained in place until a new covenant was made on the Day of Pentecost in Acts, Chapter 2.

We also recognized in the study of the Israelites' redemption that God's covenant included the spoken word and the written word (the Ten Commandments inscribed on stone). Most of us have seen illustrations of Moses descending from Mount Sinai with two tablets of stone containing the Ten Commandments. It is common to see commandments 1-5 on one tablet and 6-10 on the other tablet.

However, in my research, I have concluded that it is most likely that both tablets of stone contained all Ten Commandments. Particularly considering that the covenant was like a formal contract, in which both parties would have received a complete set of the contractual agreements. Thus, I believe that all Ten Commandments were recorded on both tablets of stone, although this cannot be confirmed in the Bible.

Both tablets of stone were placed into the Ark of the Covenant. We will explore the significance of this point when we explore the Old Testament Tabernacle in a future study.

After God made the life-changing covenant with the Israelites at Mount Sinai, they journeyed to the land that God promised to give Abraham's descendants (refer to the study on the Abrahamic Covenant). God's plan was for them to inhabit the Promised Land and live a peaceful life in the land flowing with milk and honey. Unfortunately, the Israelites chose to believe an evil report rather than having faith that God would give them the promised land. In God's anger, He caused them to wander for 40 years in the wilderness until that generation had expired. Then, God raised the next generation, who eventually conquered the Promised Land under Joshua's leadership.

SELF-REFLECTIONS:

How can you apply the discoveries of this study to your own spiritual journey?

What other events in the Bible follow the pattern that we observe in the Gospel?

How does the account of the Israelites' redemption from physical slavery compare to your redemption from spiritual slavery?

STUDY ELEVEN: *Feast of Pentecost*

OPENING PRAYER:

Heavenly Father, thank you for orchestrating the events in the Old Testament to show us your pattern of redemption. I pray that you bring spiritual revelations to each of us as we study the Feast of Pentecost. We open our minds and hearts to receive your Word. May we be strengthened and blessed as we submit our hearts to your will. We give you all the praise in the Holy Name of Jesus. Amen.

INTRODUCTION:

On the Jewish calendar, the Feast of Pentecost occurs on the sixth day of the third month, the sixth of Sivan (see Appendix A for details). The Feast of Pentecost is also referred to as the Feast of Weeks. The reason for this terminology (Feast of Weeks) will become evident as this study unfolds.

In the Greek language, *pent* means five, or a factor thereof. Consider the shape of the Pentagon in Arlington, Virginia, which has five sides, hence the proper name—Pentagon. With the Biblical account of the Feast of Pentecost, *pent* represents 50; specifically, *pente* means 50 days. You may ask, "What event in the Bible triggers the start of the 50-day count?" Allow me to expand on this.

Two significant events occurred on Sivan 6th across the span of the Bible. According to Jewish historians, the first Pentecost occurred at Mount Sinai with the giving of the Law at around 1446 BC. It was there at Mount Sinai that God spoke His Law, and then later God inscribed the Law on tablets of stone. With the Israelites' acceptance of the Law and commitment to obey the Law, a new covenant was formed, and the Dispensation of the Law began (see Appendix C and D).

Then, around AD 33, another significant event occurred in Jerusalem with the outpouring of the Holy Spirit on the Day of Pentecost, which is recorded in the book of Acts, Chapter 2. This event marked the beginning of the new Dispensation of Grace and God's new covenant by which all of mankind is subjugated today. This new covenant will remain available to those who obey the Gospel of Jesus Christ until the Dispensation of Grace closes and the final dispensation of time commences.

Within this study, we will explore and discover the similarities and differences between these two Pentecost events and the significance of the Feast of Pentecost relative to salvation for us today.

Three Jewish Feasts required pilgrimages to Jerusalem:

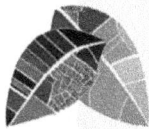

- *Feast of Passover*

- *Feast of Pentecost*

- *Feast of Tabernacles*

STUDY:

Before the Israelites met with God at Mount Sinai and heard God's voice for the first time, God asked them to make a commitment to obey the Law. In addition, God also required them to cleanse themselves.

Fill in the blanks for the scripture passage below:

EXODUS 19:4-8 (NIV)

You yourselves have seen what I did to _____, and how I _____ you on eagles' wings and _____ you to myself. Now if you _____ me fully and _____ my covenant, then out of all nations you will be my _____ possession. Although the whole earth is mine, you will be for me a _____ of priests and a _____ nation. These are the words you are to speak to the Israelites. So Moses went back and _____ the elders of the people and set before them all the words the LORD had _____ him to speak. The people all _____ together, "We will _____ everything the LORD has said." So Moses _____ their answer back to the LORD.

If the Israelites agreed to obey and keep God's covenant, what two promises did God make to them?

_____

Read Exodus 19:9-12

Before meeting with God at Mount Sinai, what were the Israelites required to do?

_____

How are these requirements related to our requirement to obey the Gospel?

_____

Before meeting with God at Mount Sinai, they were required to consecrate themselves (set apart) and to cleanse their bodies and wash their clothes. This cleansing process is symbolic of the cleansing process of repentance that is required of us today. Just as the Israelites were required to be clean before meeting with God, we likewise must *clean our hearts* through repentance before God will fill us with His Spirit.

Fill in the blanks for the scripture passage below:

LEVITICUS 23:15-17 (KJV)

And ye shall count unto you from the morrow after the sabbath, from the day that ye brought the sheaf of the wave offering; _____ sabbaths shall be complete: Even unto the morrow after the _____ sabbath shall ye number _____ days; and ye shall offer a new meat offering unto the LORD. Ye shall bring out of your habitations two wave loaves of two tenth deals; they shall be of _____ _____; they shall be baken _____ leaven; they are the first fruits unto the LORD.

How many sabbaths were to be fulfilled in verses 16 and 17?

How many total days were to be fulfilled in verse 16? (Hint: 7 sabbaths = 7 x 7 + 1)

Please note verse 17: God's plan called for *two loaves of bread*, both with *fine flour and leaven*. Recall in the study of Passover, the leaven was forbidden since it was symbolic of sin. Why, then, were they required to add the leaven back into the bread at Pentecost? Further, why were two loaves of bread specified? You will learn the significance of this requirement when we study the New Testament account of Pentecost.

To fully comprehend the starting point for the 50-day count, I suggest that you review the detailed timeline in the study of the Passover. Both the Paschal lamb and Christ were slain on Friday, Nisan 14th. The next day, Nisan 15th, would have been the Sabbath (per verse 15). Therefore, the 50-day count would have started with Nisan 16th being day 1 of the count. It may be beneficial to review the Jewish calendar in detail and notice the number of days in the first three months (see Appendix A).

The chart below details the 50-day count:

Nisan has 30 days: The 16th would start the count	During Nisan, 15 days are counted $(16^{th} - 30^{th})$: $30 - 15 = 15$	Running Total **15**
Iyyar has 29 days	During Iyyar, 29 days are counted	**44** *(29+15)*
Sivan has 30 days	During Sivan, only **six** days are needed to reach a count of 50	**50** *(6+44)*

In conclusion, the Feast of Pentecost occurred on the 6th of Sivan, which is also documented on the Jewish calendar. To summarize, 50 days after the Israelites walked out of Egypt as a free nation, God met with them at Mount Sinai and gave them the Law.

Now that we have explored the first day of Pentecost, which occurred at Mount Sinai, let's turn our attention to the day of Pentecost in the book of Acts, chapter 2. Fill in the table below and on the next page, with a summary of the verses in Acts 2:1-8:

Verse	Summary
1	
2	
3	
4	
5	
6	

Verse	Summary
7	
8	

Following this event, Peter stood with the other eleven disciples and preached the first New Testament sermon to the audience of Jews. As you may recall from a previous study, Peter was authorized by Jesus in Matthew 16:18-19 to launch the new church. A new covenant commenced at this event and is described in Acts, Chapter 2: the new covenant that was prophesied by the prophet in Jeremiah 31:31-34.

At this point in the study, I would like to bring your attention back to the Feast of Pentecost and the point I made earlier about the two loaves of bread with leaven (reference Leviticus 23:15-21): Leaven was forbidden at Passover since it is symbolic of sin.

Why, then, was the leaven added to the bread at the Feast of Pentecost?

Moreover, why were *two* loaves of bread needed?

I realize that the questions posed above are challenging, and the answers are not obvious. On a personal note, I invested a considerable amount of time searching for the correct answers. Many Bible scholars suggest answers that solve part of the questions, but leave other questions remaining. For example, some say that the two loaves of bread represented both Jews and Gentiles, or the two tablets of stone. However, this solution still does not address the addition of the leaven back into the bread.

To fully understand the two loaves of bread with leaven at the Feast of Pentecost, consider what happens to a believer's sins whenever they obey the Gospel. Just as the sins in the Old Testament were transferred to the sacrificial lambs which died and shed their blood to atone for the sins of the Israelites, whenever a believer obeys the Gospel, their sins are transferred to Christ Jesus. Once the sins are transferred to Christ, and the believer is baptized in the name of Jesus Christ, the believer *puts on Christ* (see Galatians 3:27). So then, one loaf of bread represents the sinful believer (with leaven), taking on Christ (fine flour).

Regarding the second loaf of bread with leaven, consider what transpires spiritually to Jesus whenever a believer obeys the Gospel. Here, Jesus Christ (fine flour without leaven) takes on the sin of the believer (leaven). Thus, the second loaf of bread represents Christ:

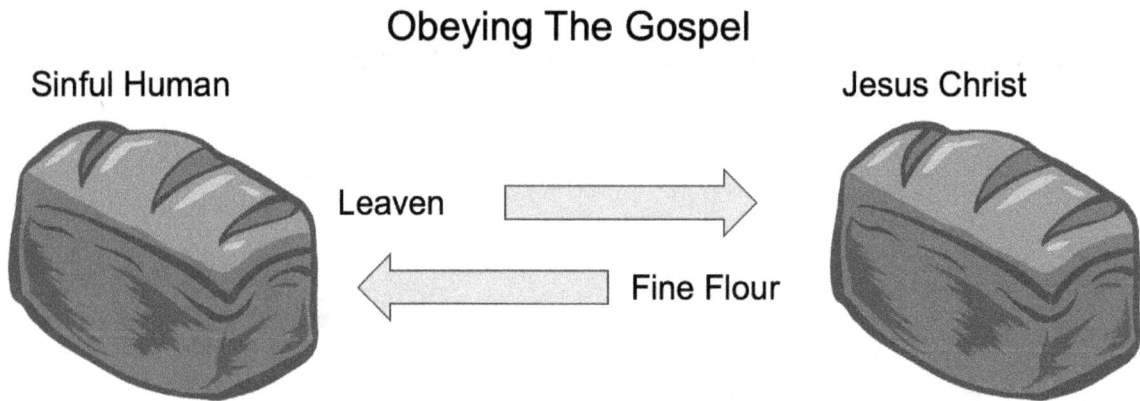

Obeying The Gospel

Sinful Human

Jesus Christ

Leaven →

← Fine Flour

Contrast the giving of the Law at Mount Sinai to the outpouring of the Holy Spirit in Acts:

How was the Pentecost at Mount Sinai symbolic of the Holy Spirit at Pentecost in Acts?

It is amazing how symbolic the first Pentecost (at Mount Sinai) is to the Pentecost in Acts. Consider the following similarities:

- Both events occurred on the 6th day of Sivan.
- Both events began a new dispensation of time.
- Both events resulted in a covenant with God.
- God descended in the visual display of fire in both cases.
- Unique sounds were heard in each case (trumpet at Mount Sinai; rushing mighty wind at Jerusalem).
- Both events resulted in resurrections (the Law resurrected the nation of Israel; the Holy Spirit resurrected the believers' spirits, new birth).

The author of the book of Hebrews contrasted these two events to show the differences. Let's explore these.

Read Hebrews 12:18-24
What event is referenced in verses 18-21?

What event is referenced in verses 22-24?

Although the two events at Pentecost had many similarities, in the Hebrew text, the author contrasts the two events to show the differences. In Hebrews 12:18-21, the author describes the frightful scene at Mount Sinai, with the mountain on fire with darkness and gloom. He further elaborates on the sound of the trumpet blasting at most likely a deafening decibel level. Then, the voice of God spoke words so powerful that the people begged to hear no more. Consider how terrifying and overwhelming this event must have been for the Israelites who were there on that day.

In verses 22-24, the author pivots the focus to Pentecost at Jerusalem in Acts, Chapter 2. In contrast to the Mount Sinai experience, the author describes a most joyful experience at the spiritual Mount Zion, the new Jerusalem, and the city of the living God. Rather than the terrifying experience at Mount Sinai, Mount Zion offers a joyful experience with angels and a new covenant relationship with Jesus Christ, our savior.

On Sivan 6th, the Israelites celebrated the giving of the Law at Mount Sinai.

The Israelites celebrated the giving of the Law on the Day of Pentecost.

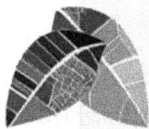

The giving of the Law at Mount Sinai occurred 50 days after the Israelites walked out of Egypt, free from slavery.

CONCLUSION:

The study of the Feast of Pentecost reminds us of just how awesome our God is. His plan was perfect in every way; every detail was planned.

First, the timing of Pentecost was the fulfillment of seven sabbaths (7 x 7 + 1) after the Israelites walked out of Egypt as free men and women. Recall from the study of Creation that seven is God's number for completion. God's message in the numerology was that the redemption was completed. In God's infinite wisdom, He also knew that the outpouring of the Holy Spirit would occur on the anniversary of Pentecost, around 1478 years after the first Pentecost. Thus, another plan of redemption was completed. Further, the Pentecost in Acts occurred 50 days after Jesus was in the tomb.

Consider the redemption of the nation of Israel; they were slaves, then free men/women. Then they were baptized in the Red Sea. Finally, the nation was resurrected on the day of Pentecost with the giving of the Law at Mount Sinai:

Israelite's Redemption

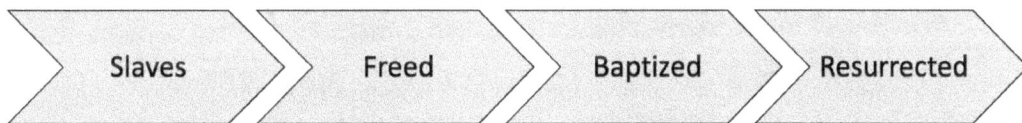

Slaves	Freed	Baptized	Resurrected

While the Law resurrected the nation of Israel and brought them into a covenant relationship with God, today, the Holy Spirit resurrects the spirits of those who obey the Gospel of Jesus Christ. Notice the parallel pattern of redemption between the Israelites' redemption and believers' redemption in our time period:

Redemption of Believers

Sinner	Forgiven	Baptized	Holy Spirit

Whenever we consider these two Pentecostal events, perhaps God was providing the Israelites with the foresight to recognize God's Messiah whenever He arrived. And then, the outpouring on the Day of Pentecost occurred on the anniversary of the giving of the Law, which should have provided another obvious clue to the Israelites that a new order of redemption had arrived.

To make sure the Israelites recognized the new covenant, God provided additional signs, such as the similarities between the two Pentecostal events. For example, there was fire descending from heaven in both cases.

Last, God specified that the Feast of Pentecost be celebrated with two loaves of bread, with leaven added to the fine flour. Recall that at the Passover, anyone who consumed leaven was *cut off* from their people; they were no longer under the Abrahamic covenant. But yet, at the Feast of Pentecost, the leaven was added to the two loaves of bread, signifying that Christ would take on the sins of the believer, while the sinner would take on Christ in baptism.

SELF-REFLECTIONS:

How did the study of Pentecost impact your view of your spiritual redemption?

How can understanding Pentecost help in leading others to Christ?

What new insights did you learn from the study of Pentecost?

STUDY TWELVE: *Feast of Tabernacles*

OPENING PRAYER:

Heavenly Father, we humble ourselves before you and acknowledge our sins and failures. In the days of old, your Holy Spirit dwelt in Tabernacles and Temples made by human hands. We thank you that we can experience your Holy Spirit dwelling in our hearts. We pray that your everlasting Word will draw us closer to you and transform us into your image. We give you all the praise in the Holy Name of Jesus. Amen.

INTRODUCTION:

The Feast of Tabernacles, which is also referenced as the Feast of Booths, occurred on the fifteenth day of the seventh month on the Jewish calendar, Tishri. See Appendix A and B for details. There is no specific historical event that coincides with the Feast of Tabernacles. Rather, the Holy Convocation of Tabernacles was considered a time for thanksgiving. At this holiday, the Jewish nation remembered and celebrated God's ever-present dwelling with them in their wilderness journey.

The word *tabernacle* originates from the Latin word *tabernaculum*, which means *tent or hut*. Combined with the Hebrew word *mishkan*, which means God's dwelling place, the resulting meaning of tabernacle is a *tent where God dwells*. However, *tabernacle* may also be used as a verb; e.g., God *tabernacled* with mankind (reference John 1:14).

After the Israelites left Egypt and journeyed to Mount Sinai, God gave Moses the detailed plans for the Tabernacle. Additionally, God provided Moses with the details for the furniture within the Tabernacle and the ceremonial laws that governed the service in the Tabernacle. Even the garments and the colors of the garments that the priests were to wear were prescribed in God's plan, which was given to Moses.

Within the Tabernacle's detailed design and ceremonial rituals, the types and shadows of Jesus and the Gospel of Jesus Christ are visible. As we explore the Feast of Tabernacles, I encourage you to be on alert to identify the many typologies that point to Christ and His Gospel.

Before we begin the study of the Feast of Tabernacles, viewing the general layout of the Tabernacle shown below will be beneficial:

Drawing of Tabernacle

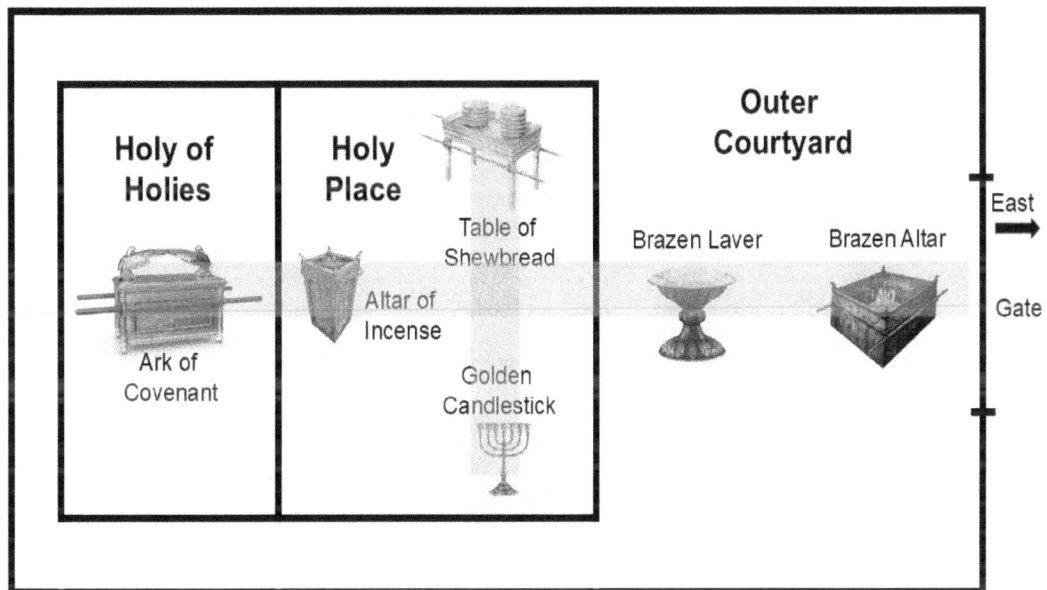

STUDY:

To begin our study, I would like to draw your attention to the diagram of the Tabernacle shown in the Introduction above. According to God's instructions to Moses, the door of the Tabernacle was to face the east; the approach to God was always from the east, moving towards the west. Directionally, this aligns with many other Biblical accounts, which involve east and west directions.

Notice the footprint of the furniture in the Tabernacle and the pattern that appears. The shape of the cross is easily recognizable in the layout of the furniture.

Next, notice the three separate areas. The Outer Court was not covered, and everyone was allowed access. The furniture in this area was covered in brass, which is an inferior quality of metal in comparison to gold, signifying the presence of humanity.

Both the Holy Place and Holy of Holies were covered with four layers of material. Within these two areas, all the furniture was covered in gold. Only the priests and the high priest could access the Holy Place to perform their duties. Then, the Holy of Holies could only be accessed by the high priest, and only on one day per year—the Day of Atonement, which was Tishri 10th.

BRAZEN ALTAR:
Read Exodus 27:1-8, Exodus 30:10

BRAZEN LAVER:
Read Exodus 30:18-21

ARK OF THE COVENANT:
Read Exodus 25:10-22

What was the first article of furniture that the worshippers encountered whenever they entered the Tabernacle?

What was the purpose of the Brazen Altar?

What would happen if a high priest did not wash in the Brazen Laver before entering the Holy of Holies?

Why was this important?

At what article of furniture would God meet and commune with the high priest?

The first article of furniture encountered by those entering the Tabernacle was the Brazen Altar. It was here that the process of atonement began with the slaying of the sacrificial animal. Recall the first step in the pattern of the Gospel of Jesus Christ. The death of the sacrificial animals in the Tabernacle was a type and shadow of the death of the future Lamb of God: the Messiah.

Next, they would encounter the Brazen Laver. The high priest would wash his hands and feet in the Brazen Laver, symbolizing both his physical and spiritual cleansing before proceeding into the presence of God. If this step was not followed, he would perish in the presence of God. Why would God slay them? Because they were not spiritually clean, they were not *righteous* before God.

The Holy of Holies was the most sacred place in the Tabernacle. It was here that the Ark of the Covenant rested. The very presence of God resided here, hovering over the Mercy Seat. On the Day of Atonement, the high priest would enter the presence of God in the Holy of Holies to make the annual atonement for himself and his family. And then he would enter a second time to atone for the sins of the nation of Israel.

Inside the Ark of the Covenant, there were three items (reference Hebrews 9:4):

Item in the Ark of the Covenant	Representation
Two Tablets of Stone • Ten Commandments	God's Law
Aaron's Rod • Numbers 17:1-8 • Numbers 18:6-7	God's Authority
Golden Vase with Manna • From Journey in Wilderness	God's Provision

How are these three articles of furniture (Brazen Altar, Brazen Laver, and Ark of the Covenant) symbolic of the Gospel of Jesus Christ?

_____

_____

Once again, the pattern of the Gospel of Jesus Christ becomes visible as we focus on the articles and furniture and their use in atoning for the sins of Israel. First, we see the death of the sacrificial animal, which is a type and shadow of the future death of the Messiah. Then, there was the washing in the Brazen Laver, which is symbolic of the spiritual cleansing that comes with baptism.

Recall in the study on "Obeying the Gospel of Jesus Christ," we established that baptism is symbolically being buried with Christ (reference Romans 6:4). Only after the high priest completed the death of the sacrifice, and symbolic baptism with the washing in the Brazen Laver could he enter into the Holy of Holies and meet with God and experience His refreshing presence (a type of resurrection).

The fire at the Brazen Altar came directly from God.

(Leviticus 9:24)

God commanded the Israelites never to allow the fire to go out.

(Leviticus 6:12-13)

Now, let us update the table that tabulates the various Biblical accounts that reflect the pattern of the Gospel of Jesus Christ.

Complete the last row in the table below with the information you learned from the study of the Brazen Altar, Brazen Laver, and Ark of the Covenant:

GOSPEL	DEATH	BURIAL	RESURRECTION
Jesus	Crucified	Buried	Rose again 3rd day
Believer Obeying the Gospel	Repents Dying of Carnal Nature	Baptized Buried with Christ Jesus	Receives the Holy Spirit Spiritual Birth
Noah and His Family	Repentance God repented for creating man	Burial Flood buried the Earth	Resurrection New life without sin after the Flood
Israelite Slaves Redemption from Slavery	Death of Paschal Lamb Means to Freedom, Blood saved them from the wrath of God	Baptism Baptized in the Red Sea and the cloud	Received the Law Resurrected nation with life-changing Law
Tabernacle			

I have included a completed table of the pattern (above), which is available in Appendix H.

There are several other articles of furniture that were placed in the Holy Place. Each of these has a spiritual significance that is worthy of our exploration.

GOLDEN CANDLESTICK:
Read Exodus 25:31-37
Read Exodus 27:20-21

How is the Golden Candlestick a type and shadow of Jesus Christ?

Keeping in mind that the Holy Place and Holy of Holies were completely covered, the only light within the Holy Place was illuminated from the Golden Candlestick (KJV). The term *candlestick* is somewhat of a misnomer in our vernacular since olive oil was burned rather than candles. In today's terminology, we would label this as a lamp or lantern. In some Bible translations, the more appropriate term *Golden Lampstand* is recorded.

Christians understand that Jesus is the *light of the world* (reference John 8:12). The priests ministering in the Tabernacle walked in the light from the Golden Candlestick just as Christians today walk in the light of the Spirit. Without this light, the priests would have been in complete darkness.

As we consider the design of the Golden Candlestick, we see six branches. Recall that the number six represents man (created on the sixth day of Creation). Then, there is the additional (seventh) stem in the center of the Golden Candlestick, bringing the total lamps to seven, which represents God and His completeness. Therefore, the design of the Golden Candlestick declared Jesus Christ in His humanity and His divinity:

- Jesus Christ was 100% human.
- Jesus Christ was 100% Deity (God).

The oil burned in the lamps was a spiritual representation of the Holy Spirit. Do you recall the Parable of the Virgins found in Matthew 25:1-13? In this parable, only the wise virgins, whose lamps were full of oil, made it to the marriage supper. The foolish virgins, who did not have enough oil, missed out on the marriage supper and were not allowed in.

TABLE OF SHEWBREAD:
Read Exodus 25:23-30
Read Leviticus 24:5-9

What did the 12 loaves of shewbread represent?

The term "shewbread" in Hebrew is *lehem haPanim,* which literally translates to *bread of the faces.* Shewbread is also referred to as the *presence bread* because God commanded that the bread be always present before Him. The shewbread was also a reminder to the priests of God's blessings and provisions for the nation of Israel.

We also learned in reading this text that there were 12 loaves of shewbread; each loaf represented one of the 12 tribes of Israel. The loaves were arranged in two rows of six each. This same pattern (two rows of six) is repeated with the two stones, which were placed on the shoulders of the priests' garments (to be explored later).

Although not specifically stated in the Bible, it is believed that the shewbread was unleavened, which would align with the unleavened bread prescribed in the Feast of Passover.

According to Jewish historians (see reference below), the shewbread was baked the morning of the Sabbath and set out on the Table of Shewbread. The 12 loaves of shewbread remained there until the following Sabbath. Once the shewbread was replaced, the old shewbread was given to the priests for their consumption.

Jewish Encyclopedia:

Frankincense was placed on each of the rows of shewbread, which was a symbol of the deity. Frankincense was also one of the gifts that the Magi brought to the child Jesus (reference Matthew 2:11).

TABLE OF INCENSE:
Read Exodus 30:1-8

What was the purpose of burning incense at the Table of Incense?

We read in Revelation 8:3-4 that the prayers of the saints are as incense before God. Burning of incense at the Table of Incense in the Tabernacle represented the continual prayers and praises of the Israelites to God. The rising smoke was a visual display of the prayers and the Israelites' desire to be pleasing to God.

   Only the coals from the Brazen Altar were used to burn the incense. This fire was ignited directly by God and could never be extinguished (reference Leviticus 6:12-13 and Leviticus 9:24).

FEAST OF TABERNACLES:

Read Leviticus 23:33-43
Why did the Israelites dwell in booths (tents) during the Feast of Tabernacles?

Why were their tent flaps (openings) always facing the Tabernacle?

As a way of remembering God dwelling with them during their wilderness journey, the Israelites dwelt in tents during the seven days celebrating the Feast of Tabernacles. Their tents were arranged so that the tent flaps always faced the Tabernacle, so the first thing they saw each morning, and the last thing they saw each evening, was the Tabernacle. Jewish historical accounts suggest that the Israelites also set up numerous lanterns around the perimeter of the Tabernacle so that the Tabernacle was illuminated and visible day and night during the seven days commemorating the Feast of Tabernacles.

Fill in the blanks for the key passage below.

JOHN 2:19 (KJV)

Jesus answered and said unto them, destroy this _____, and in three days I will raise it up.

Why did Jesus refer to Himself as the Temple (Tabernacle)?

_____

_____

_____

CONCLUSION:

What an amazing account of redemption! The Israelite people, descendants of Abraham with whom God made a covenant, were delivered from slavery, baptized in the Red Sea, and resurrected to become the only nation on earth with a covenant relationship with God Almighty. Then, God provided His people with a way to atone for their sins with the Tabernacle and the ceremonial law.

Israelites' Journey

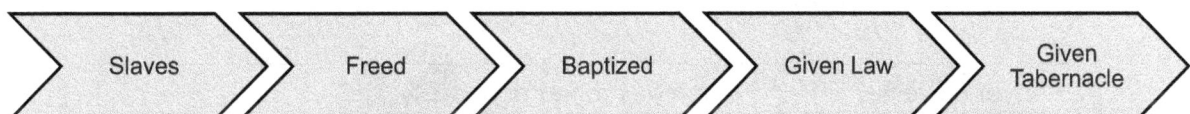

Slaves → Freed → Baptized → Given Law → Given Tabernacle

The Tabernacle and the articles of furniture, along with the ceremonial law, provided the Israelites a way to atone for their sins. By the shedding of the blood of sacrificial animals and the washing in the Brazen Laver (a type of baptism), the high priest was free to atone for their sins in the presence of God before the Ark of the Covenant. It is not a surprise that the method for their atonement mirrored the pattern of the Gospel of Jesus Christ.

As we have seen, this same Gospel pattern is repeated time and again across various accounts in the Bible. Perhaps this is God's way of pointing humanity to the Messiah and His sacrifice, as well as the steps required for obeying His Gospel. By giving us numerous examples of the Gospel pattern, the method of obeying His Gospel becomes increasingly obvious.

The other articles of furniture in the Tabernacle also pointed to the Messiah:

- Golden Candlestick (Menorah) – Christ Jesus
    - Jesus is the light of the world
    - Jesus is both human and God
    - Holy Spirit as oil in lamps
- Table of Shewbread—His provision
- Table of Incense—Praises of His people

There are many more details involving the Tabernacle that have spiritual significance. For example, even the colors used in the Tabernacle's sides, door, and veil pointed to Christ Jesus (reference Exodus 26):

Color	Representation	Jesus Christ
Blue	Heaven / Divinity	Son of God
Purple	Royalty	King of Kings and Lord of Lords
Red	Humanity / Blood	Sacrificial Lamb of God

As mentioned previously, the Holy Place and the Holy of Holies were completely covered with four layers of material (reference Exodus 26):

1st Layer (lower)	Linen described above
2nd Layer	Goat's skin (sacrifice)
3rd Layer	Ram's skin, stained red (sacrifice)
4th (outer)	Seal's skin, to hide the Glory of the Tabernacle

The priests' garments contained the same colors as mentioned above. Additionally, their ephod contained golden strands woven into the colorful linen, which denoted that God highly valued them. Below is an artist's rendition of the priests' garments as described in Exodus 28:

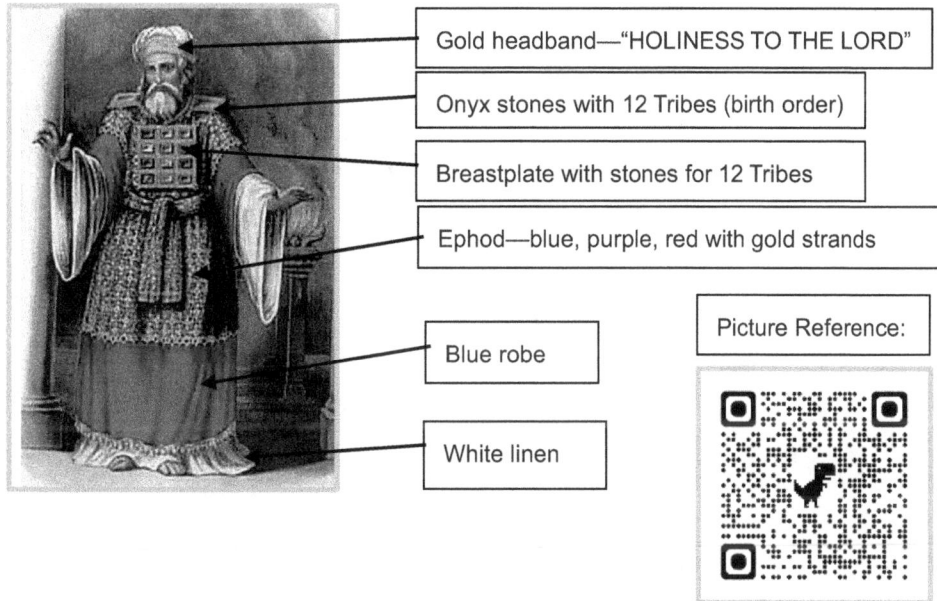

Gold headband—"HOLINESS TO THE LORD"

Onyx stones with 12 Tribes (birth order)

Breastplate with stones for 12 Tribes

Ephod—blue, purple, red with gold strands

Blue robe

White linen

Picture Reference:

The two onyx stones on the shoulders of the priests' garments were engraved with the birth order of the 12 sons of Israel; six on each side. Onyx is believed to represent the stone of Joseph. Therefore, the use of onyx is symbolic of Joseph's role in rescuing the Israelites from the great seven-year famine.

As we contemplate the significance of the Feast of Tabernacles, be aware that there is much more to come. In the final dispensation of time (Kingdom Reign), God will *tabernacle* with humankind once again (reference Revelation 21:3).

Urim and Thummim were oracles of God—placed in the pockets of priests' ephods. Little is known about these materials or how they were used to communicate with God.

Exodus 28

SELF-REFLECTIONS:

In what way did the study of the Feast of Tabernacles increase your knowledge of God?

How does your personal spiritual journey mirror that of the ceremonial law found in the study of the Feast of Tabernacles?

What new knowledge did you gain from this study that will help in your spiritual walk with God?

STUDY THIRTEEN:
Repentance and Forgiveness

OPENING PRAYER:

Heavenly Father, thank you for creating us with a spirit and a living soul. As we study your Word, let each of us feel conviction for our sins and humble ourselves in repentance. We prepare our minds and our hearts to receive your Word. Let the power of your Word transform each of us through this study. May your everlasting Word strengthen our faith and trust in you. We give you all the praise in the Holy Name of Jesus. Amen.

INTRODUCTION:

Back in the early 1990s, we gifted our son a Nintendo Game System for Christmas. I'll never forget the first time the Mario man fell into a deep cavern, ending the game, and hearing that horrible tune that sounded, informing my son that he had lost. My son was so upset until he understood that there was a reset button. Voila! Mario was once again ready to jump over the same cavern as if nothing had ever happened. No matter how many times my son lost, he had infinite opportunities to play the game again.

Have you ever made such a disaster of a situation that you wished you could go back in time and try again? Where is the *reset button* in life when you need one? I am sure everyone would agree with me that our actions and words have consequences in the natural world. Sometimes our mistakes can be corrected or at least the effects softened. However, they often cannot be corrected. We are forced to suffer the consequences of some mistakes.

Fortunately for humanity, when it comes to spiritual matters, God has provided us with a type of *reset button* called repentance. When a person truly repents of their sins, God is just to forgive and forget, giving the person a second chance (1 John 1:9), a third chance, or a fourth chance. Of course, we should never tempt God by taking advantage of His mercy by assuming we can continue living a life of sin.

We explored the concept of repentance in the study on "Obeying the Gospel of Jesus Christ". In this study, we will go even deeper into the study of repentance.

Here are a few words and definitions that will become beneficial to you as we explore the principle of repentance:

REPENTANCE:
- Acknowledgment of sins
- Godly sorrow for sins
- To turn away from sin (and turn towards God)
- To commit to a righteous lifestyle
- To seek God's forgiveness

MERCY:
- God's compassion and kindness
- When due punishment is forgiven

GRACE:
- God's unmerited favor, kindness, or love
- A gift not earned or deserved

According to these definitions, *mercy* is *not receiving* the punishment deserved, whereas *grace* is *receiving* a gift or favor that is *not* merited. God's grace is extended to all of humanity (reference Titus 2:11). God's mercy is granted to those who repent of their sins and turn to Him.

Is repentance essential for salvation, and can a person obey the Gospel of Jesus Christ without repentance? Rather than provide answers to these questions here, let us turn to the Bible for the answers.

STUDY:

Read Matthew 3:1-11

What message did John the Baptist preach in the wilderness?

Why did John the Baptist baptize his followers?

What was John's warning to the Pharisees and Sadducees in verses 9-10?

Isaiah prophesied of John the Baptist in Isaiah 40:3-4:

> *The voice of him that crieth in the wilderness, Prepare ye the way of the LORD,*
> *make straight in the desert a highway for our God.*
> *Every valley shall be exalted, and every mountain and hill shall be made low:*
> *and the crooked shall be made straight, and the rough places plain:*
> *Isaiah 40:3-4 (KJV)*

John, born of the tribe of Levi, was the fulfillment of Isaiah's prophecy. Many living at that time must have thought of John as a wild man. He wore a robe of camel hair with a leather girdle, eating off the land. Yet his message was powerful and compelling. "Repent ye, for the kingdom of heaven is at hand," (Matthew 3:2 [KJV]) was his message. For those who would listen and obey, John persuaded them to be baptized unto repentance. Just to be completely clear with his followers, he proclaimed that One mightier than him would come after him with another baptism.

The Jewish religious leaders of that day went out to observe and challenge John's message and authority. In our previous studies, we established that the nation of Israel was in a covenant relationship with God with the giving of the Law at Mount Sinai, and they were also heirs to the Abrahamic covenant. As such, the Jewish leaders were living under the false assumption that their heritage protected them. John's response to them is recorded in Matthew 3:9-10. His commandment was the same for these religious leaders as for everyone: REPENT! He even went a step further to warn them that the "axe is laid unto the root of the tree". The fulfillment of the Law was at hand, and a new covenant would bring a change to mankind's approach to God.

Keeping in mind that Jesus had not yet died, been buried, and risen from the dead, John could not preach the Gospel and God's full plan for salvation. However, he could give them a head start by helping them through the repentance process and introducing the principle of baptism to his followers.

Fill in the blanks of the key passages below:

MATTHEW 4:17 (KJV)

From that time Jesus began to preach, and to say, _____: for the kingdom of heaven is at hand.

MARK 6:12 (KJV)

And they [disciples] went out, and preached that men should _____.

What consistent message did Jesus and His disciples preach?

_____

_____

_____

Read Luke 13:3 / 5
Read Acts 2:38-39
Read 2 Peter 3:9
Read 2 Thessalonians 1:7-9
Read I Corinthians 15:31

According to these scriptures, what will happen to those who do not repent?

In the context of the Bible, what does the word "perish" mean?

Is repentance of sins essential for salvation?

What did Paul mean by stating, "I die daily?"

Before Jesus' sacrifice at Calvary, there was a consistent message from John the Baptist, Jesus, and His disciples: "Repent, for the kingdom of heaven is at hand". Jesus also made it crystal clear in His preaching that those who do not repent would perish. We see evidence of this reality again in Peter's writing: either *repent* or perish. Without a doubt, repentance for sins is essential for salvation.

Recall from the study on "Obeying the Gospel of Jesus Christ." *Repentance* aligns with the death of Jesus Christ since one's carnal nature is *crucified with Christ* whenever a person truly repents of their sins (reference Romans 6:6). Paul provides us a perfect example of daily repentance in 1 Corinthians 15:31 regarding his practice of dying daily.

Read Colossians 2:11-13

Read Acts 3:19

Read 1 John 1:9

What happens to a person's sins whenever they repent?

_____

_____

According to these scriptures, when one confesses their sins to God and repents, God is just to forgive their sins. In the spirit realm, the blood of Jesus atones for the sins of the believer who confesses and repents of their sins. For those who have experienced the repentance process and felt the overwhelming feeling that comes with God's forgiveness, it typically results in a highly emotional sense of peace.

Fill in the blanks:

MATTHEW 6:14-15 (KJV)

For if ye _____ men their trespasses, your heavenly Father will also _____ you: But if ye _____ not men their trespasses, neither will your Father _____ your trespasses.

What act of forgiveness is required of a believer before God will forgive their sins?

_____

_____

_____

I have worked with many new believers who struggle with repentance. Some new believers do not experience the peace of forgiveness from God after they have repented of their sins. Usually, the problem is that they are harboring unresolved forgiveness for those who have seriously wronged them. Unless a person resolves these issues and releases the offenses to God, they simply cannot move forward in their spiritual growth. If you are in this situation, or if you know someone struggling with this situation, I offer you the following advice to those seeking to forgive others of their offenses:

- You do not have to reconcile with the person who has harmed you.
- You do not have to pretend that the offense was of no consequence or that it did not hurt you. It is acceptable to acknowledge that the offense hurt and was not fair.
- You do, however, have to reach a point where you can ask God to forgive them of the offense (s). Just as Christ prayed for those nailing his hands and feet to the cross, He prayed, "Father, forgive them … "

As you consider the principles of repentance, keep in mind that the primary objective is to gain forgiveness for your sins.

CONCLUSION:

Let us review some of the key points that we have established so far:

- The punishment for sin is death.
- Shedding of blood is required to atone for sins.
- Repentance is symbolic of death; it is the crucifixion of the sinful nature.
- Death and repentance are synonymous.

As we have seen throughout these studies, the first step in the pattern of redemption is death/repentance. Across the span of the Bible, we observe this pattern repeated. According to the account of Noah and the great flood, it began with God repenting and His decision to rid the world of wickedness. Likewise, the Paschal lambs in Egypt were slain, and the blood was placed on the doorposts, which was symbolic of atonement for the households of the Israelites. Under the Dispensation of the Law, sacrificial animals were slain, which was the first step in the atonement process. Ultimately, the perfect human sacrifice died, shedding His blood for the sins of the entire world.

The first step in the pattern of redemption is undeniable. What does this mean for us today? For all who believe in Jesus Christ and His Gospel, the first step towards redemption and salvation is repentance, which is the crucifixion of the carnal, sinful nature. Just as the Israelites were required to remove all residue of unleavened bread from their quarters during the Passover period, likewise, our repentance must include an evaluation of our homes, lifestyles, relationships, social media input, etc. Everything unpleasing to God must be eliminated from our lives.

As part of the repentance process, a believer must also forgive others. Otherwise, their sins will not be forgiven. To simplify the principle of repentance and forgiveness/atonement of sins, consider the following:

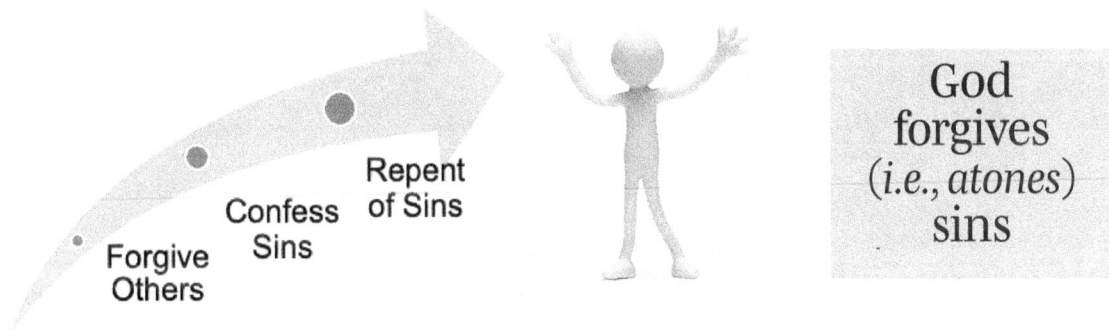

Repent
of Sins

Confess
Sins

Forgive
Others

God
forgives
(*i.e., atones*)
sins

Keep in mind that the ultimate goal is to have your sins forgiven! Even though God expects everyone to strive for a sin-free life, we are still human and will occasionally make a mistake. Therefore, it is imperative that we form a daily regimen of prayer, which must include repenting for sins and a continuation of dying away of our carnal nature. Remember Paul's example to us? He recorded that he *died daily*. He crucified his sinful nature daily.

SELF-REFLECTIONS:

In what areas of your life has someone hurt you? Have you forgiven them?

What lifestyle changes are you willing to make to have a closer relationship with God?

How would you describe your walk with God today regarding the forgiveness of sins? Check all that apply.

- ☐ The offenses of my enemies are forgiven
- ☐ I am aware of my sins and have confessed them to God.
- ☐ I have fully repented of all sins.
- ☐ I have peace from God's forgiveness.
- ☐ I employ a daily regimen of repentance.

Repentance is essential for Salvation!

STUDY FOURTEEN: *Water Baptism*

OPENING PRAYER:

Heavenly Father, we thank you for the good news of the Gospel of Jesus Christ. Thank you for making a way for us to be buried with you in baptism. We open our minds and our hearts to receive your Word. Let understanding and new revelations come to each of us through this study. May your Word strengthen our faith and trust in you. We give you all the praise in the Holy Name of Jesus. Amen.

INTRODUCTION:

I remember the day I baptized a new believer whom I had been mentoring. I gave him several Bible studies to understand how to obey the Gospel for salvation. Circumstances led us to conduct the baptism in a friend's hot tub. It was during the cold winter season, and it was much too cold to consider using my friend's pool. I knew the new believer was tall; I just didn't appreciate how tall! As I buried him under the water in baptism, his head landed on the steps right below the water surface in the hot tub. There I was trying to get him completely under the water, and his head would not go under.

Finally, we aborted the baptism and started over with him kneeling in the water. What an embarrassing event! Fortunately, he was not injured in the process. Perhaps you have experienced a comical baptism event that causes you to smile whenever you reminisce.

Baptism is not a new concept, but rather has been in practice for thousands of years. The Jewish nation practiced ceremonial cleansings, with evidence recorded in Leviticus and Exodus. One sect of Jews, the Essenes, practiced a morning ritual of cleansing before their prayer time. Some historians believe that John the Baptist was from the sect of Essenes, who were from the tribe of Levi, with a mission to preserve the priesthood.

When John the Baptist came on the scene, preaching repentance and baptism unto repentance, the concept of baptism was not completely foreign to his followers of that day. There were numerous *mikvehs* (Hebrew word for baths) around the Temple Mount in Jerusalem. However, John chose to baptize his followers in the Jordan River. John's baptism of repentance was preparatory, and he declared to his followers that One was to come after him with another baptism.

Even Jesus was baptized by John as an act of obedience to His Messianic calling. John witnessed the Spirit descend upon Jesus like a dove and heard the voice of God declaring Jesus to be His son. (reference Mark 1:4-11) However, John was only a forerunner to Jesus; thus, John's baptism became obsolete with the outpouring of the Holy Spirit on the Day of Pentecost (Acts 2).

As we discussed in Study Six, the word baptism comes from the Greek word *baptizo* (root word *bapto)*, which means to immerse or submerge. Therefore, by definition, the act of baptism should involve immersion in water as a declaration of being symbolically buried with Christ.

In my experience, the concept of baptism among the Christian community is surrounded by great controversy. Some of the many debates that I've encountered regarding baptism are:

- Is baptism essential for salvation?
- Is immersion required, or is *sprinkling* with water sufficient?
- Can infants receive eternal salvation by baptism?
- What name or titles should be called upon during baptism?

Unfortunately, many opinions regarding baptism tend to separate believers into many religious denominations. The goal of this study is to explore the biblical approach to water baptism and discover the truth.

STUDY:

IS BAPTISM ESSENTIAL FOR SALVATION?
Read Mark 16:16
Read John 3:1-6

According to Mark 16:16, is baptism necessary for salvation?

In Jesus' conversation with Nicodemus, what two births are required for entry into the kingdom of God?

What is the meaning of the term "born of the water"?

In Mark's writing, it is clear that believing and baptism are two of the essential elements required for salvation. Believing is an obvious first step. Without believing in the Gospel of Jesus Christ, a person will never take steps to obey His Gospel. As we have already established, repentance is also a necessary step that should precede baptism.

Nicodemus met with Jesus in the secrecy of the night to inquire about His ministry. Jesus made it clear to Nicodemus that being born again of the water and the Spirit was required for entry into the kingdom of God (salvation). Jesus' comments seemed to confuse Nicodemus since the gift of the Holy Spirit had not yet been given. However, for us today, we have the benefit of understanding that being "born of the water" refers to baptism.

Fill in the blanks:

ACTS 2:38-39 (KJV)

Then Peter said unto them, "Repent, and be _____ _____ every one of you in the name of _____ _____ for the remission of sins, and ye shall receive the gift of the _____ _____."

What was Peter's message to the people?

_____

_____

Whose name was to be called on during baptism?

_____

_____

After the outpouring of the Holy Spirit in Acts 2, Peter stood with the other disciples and preached the first Apostolic message to the audience of Jews who were gathered in Jerusalem to celebrate the Feast of Pentecost. In verse 38 of Acts 2, Peter issues a command that summarizes the key steps necessary for salvation (refer to the study on "Obeying the Gospel"). His commandment further supports the overwhelming evidence that baptism is indeed essential for salvation.

If you are wondering where Peter received his authority to launch the New Testament church, refer to Matthew 16:15-19; Jesus gave Peter _the keys to the kingdom of heaven._

JESUS' COMMANDMENT REGARDING BAPTISM

Fill in the blanks:

MATTHEW 28:19 (KJV)
Go ye therefore, and teach all nations, baptizing them in the name of the _____, and of the _____, and of the _____ _____.
Notice in this reading, the name is singular, not plural. Therefore, we should seek the one name that fulfills the roles of all three titles described in this verse:

- Father
- Son
- Holy Ghost

NAME OF THE FATHER:

Read John:10:30

Read John 5:43

In whose name did Jesus come?

What is the name of the Father?

NAME OF THE SON:

Read Luke 1:31

What is the name of the Son?

NAME OF THE HOLY GHOST (SPIRIT):

Read John 14:26

Read John 15:26

What is the name of the Holy Ghost?

Fill in the blanks:

ISAIAH 9:6 (KJV)

For unto us a child is born, unto us a _____ is given: and the government shall be upon His shoulder: and His _____ shall be called Wonderful, _____, The mighty _____, the everlasting _____, the Prince of Peace.

Whose birth is prophesied in this scripture?

From Isaiah's prophecy of the Messiah, we learn that the name of the Messiah (Jesus) will represent:

- The Counselor, which is the Holy Ghost (reference John 14:26)
- The Mighty God
- The Everlasting Father

Once again, we have established that the name of Jesus represents the role of not only the Son of God but also the Holy Spirit and the Everlasting Father.

So then, what is the one, singular name that is referenced in the Great Commission (Matthew 28:19)? It is the name "Jesus!" The name of Jesus is the only name that represents all the roles listed in the Great Commission.

WHAT DOES BAPTISM SYMBOLIZE?

Read Romans 6:3-6
Read Galatians 3:27-29
Read Colossians 2:11-13

Fill in the blanks:
Being baptized is symbolic of being _____ with Christ. Whenever a person is _____ into Christ, he/she _____ on Christ.

From these scriptures, we learn that baptism is symbolic of burial. Jesus died and was buried; therefore, we must also be buried in baptism with Jesus. In Galatians 3:27, the scripture states that whenever a person is baptized into Christ, they *put on* Christ. In Romans 6:5, the scripture is presented in a *conditional context* (per language: *rules of structure*) denoted by the use of the word "if."

Therefore, *if* a person has been planted (baptized) together in the likeness of His death, *then* they will be in the likeness of His resurrection. We can likewise conclude that if a person *is not* planted together in the likeness of His death, then they will not be in the likeness of His resurrection.

If	Baptized in Christ	Share in His resurrection
If Not	Baptized	Does NOT share in His resurrection

HOW MANY BAPTISMS ARE THERE BIBLICALLY?

Read Ephesians 4:5

Read Acts 4:12

Read Colossians 3:17

How many baptisms are acceptable according to these scriptures?

What name was given to mankind, in which we should do all things?

According to Ephesians 4:5, there is only one acceptable baptism. What is the one and only correct baptism? These scriptures suggest that baptism in the name of Jesus is the one and only acceptable formula for baptism.

HOW DID THE APOSTLES BAPTIZE?

Read Acts 8:14-17: Conversion of Samaritan believers.

Read Acts 10:44-47: Conversion of Cornelius' household.

Read Acts 19:1-6: Conversion of believers at Ephesus.

In these three accounts, what "name" were the believers baptized into?

The disciples understood Jesus' commandment in Matthew 28:19 and obeyed his commandment; they baptized in the name of Jesus. Notice in the account of the believers in Ephesus, their first baptism was unto repentance (by John the Baptist). Therefore, they were baptized a second time in the name of Jesus.

CONCLUSION:

As we have seen in other Biblical accounts, burial/baptism is an integral part of the pattern of redemption. Recall the study of Noah, where Peter records in 1 Peter 3:21-22, the water from the flood was a type of baptism. Likewise, we learned in 1 Corinthians 10:1-3, the account of Moses and the Israelites' crossing of the Red Sea was symbolic of baptism.

In Acts, Chapter 2, the Bible records that 3,000 believers were baptized on the day of Pentecost. How were so many people baptized in such a short period of time? Historical accounts reveal that the many mikvehs around Jerusalem were utilized to accomplish the thousands of baptisms. Based on Peter's sermon on that day, those baptized were baptized in the name of Jesus. Further in the New Testament, we read the accounts of other believers being baptized in the name of Jesus. Clearly, the early church only baptized believers in the name of Jesus.

Have you ever wondered or even questioned religious doctrine? I remember a time in my life when I decided to set aside my previous religious teaching and seek the truth from a Biblical perspective. During this *spiritual revolution*, I recall studying the Bible to understand baptism. Using one of my favorite Bible software programs, I searched for the word "baptize" and all the synonyms (baptized, baptism, etc.). After reading these 100 references on baptism, I concluded that baptism by immersion was important, while the formula of words spoken was less important. However, I remained somewhat uncomfortable with this conclusion based on Ephesians 4:5: One baptism.

On one of our family outings in Houston, we were planning to have lunch at one of our favorite spots: The Strawberry Patch, on Westheimer. If you have ever experienced Westheimer traffic, you understand how chaotic it can be. We finally arrived at our destination, only to find that the restaurant had closed and another was now occupying the building. Not wanting to venture back into the traffic, we conceded to dining at the new restaurant. Whenever we were seated and looked at the menu, I knew we were in trouble; the prices were extreme. Not wishing to make a scene and leave, we decided to suffer through the meal.

My son was around 10-11 years old at that time. He was old enough to be in the "smart-mouth" stage. Attempting to be discreet, I leaned over and whispered to him, "Son, tell me what you are planning to order?" My goal was to direct him to the least expensive menu selection.

My son's response was, "What you are planning to order."

I thought, *No! Now is not the time for him to get smart with me and start mocking!* So I repeated my commandment for the second time, "No, no, no. Tell me what you are going to order."

His reply was like the first reply: "What you are going to order."

At this point, the Holy Spirit whispered in a still, small voice: "Matthew 28:19." On the drive home, I reflected on my interaction with my son, and the sudden thought of Matthew 28:19 that had come in that moment. Then the understanding came to me. When the titles "Father, Son, and Holy Ghost" are used in baptism, Jesus' commandment is being *repeated* rather than being *obeyed*. Therefore, it makes perfect sense that the apostles were baptizing in His name.

Then, I wondered when the formula for baptism changed to the titles versus the biblical formula of baptism *in the name of Jesus*. My research led to the Council of Nicaea, where 200-plus priests and bishops came together in Nicaea (Turkey) and debated various issues. They concluded and declared in AD 325 that the correct formula for baptism was in the titles "Father, Son, and Holy Ghost" and not the name of Jesus. One source of this information is included below for your reference in the QR code below.

I realize that the Biblical evidence presented in this study may not align with your religious teaching. You have free will, of course, to decide how you will react to this information. As you consider your options, I ask that you pray and ask God to guide you with your decision. After all, your very soul could be at risk.

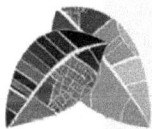

Water Baptism in the Name of Jesus is essential for Salvation.

SELF-REFLECTIONS:

What were the main takeaways from this study?

What additional questions do you have regarding baptism? List them below:

What further research are you planning to pursue regarding baptism?

STUDY FIFTEEN: *The Gift of the Holy Spirit*

OPENING PRAYER:

Heavenly Father, we thank you for the good news of the Gospel of Jesus Christ. Thank you for the gift of your Holy Spirit to all who obey your Gospel. We open our minds and our hearts to receive your Word. Let understanding and new revelations come to each of us through this study. May your Word strengthen our faith and trust in you. We give you all the praise in the Holy Name of Jesus. Amen.

INTRODUCTION:

Thinking back on Christmastime, when our children were young, I remember having all the gifts wrapped with festive paper and bows arranged artistically under the Christmas tree. It never failed that our children would beg to open just one gift the night before the big day. They could not wait until Christmas morning. Invariably, their mother and I would eventually give in and allow them to open just one gift.

I have witnessed many friends receiving gifts from close friends and loved ones. Yet, I have never observed anyone refusing to accept a gift. Instead, the recipient of the gift always seems eager and excited to rip off the paper to see what awaits them. Perhaps Peter understood how people react when presented with gifts from loved ones. With this insight, he presented the infilling of the Holy Spirit as a *gift* from God (reference Acts 2:38-39).

Across time, generation after generation awaited, with much anticipation, the coming of the Messiah and the salvation that He would deliver. Many read and believed the prophecies that confirmed with certainty the coming of the Messiah. They could only wait, hope, and pray, as they imagined how great His salvation would be.

Then Jesus arrived: The Son of God, The Messiah, the Appointed Flesh of God. Because of His humble birth and lowly family life, many at that time did not acknowledge Him. Instead, they patiently continued to await a great king, a great warrior similar to King David. They were looking for someone to deliver them from the Roman occupation.

If only those of that era could have recognized God's pattern of redemption. It had been modeled for them throughout the Old Testament. Then it was being played out again right before their eyes: the death, the burial, and the resurrection of Jesus. God, in His perfect way, aligned the dates of Jesus' triumphal entry into Jerusalem and His death to the dates of the selection and slaying of the Paschal lambs back in Egypt. It is no surprise that the outpouring of the Holy Spirit in the book of Acts occurred on the anniversary of the Mount Sinai event. It was exactly 50 days after Jesus was buried (reference the study on the Feast of Pentecost).

The account of the outpouring of the Holy Spirit in Acts chapter 2 has been highly debated among the various Christian denominations. Some of the key questions regarding the infilling of the Holy Spirit are:

- How does the infilling of the Holy Spirit in Acts impact us today?
- Is the same gift of the Holy Spirit that was poured out in Acts still available to us in the 21st century?
- Why do we need the Holy Spirit?
- Is receiving the gift of the Holy Spirit essential for salvation?

Let us explore the Bible for answers to these questions in the following scripture study.

STUDY:

OLD TESTAMENT PROPHECY

Fill in the blanks for the scripture mentioned below:

JOEL 2:28-29 (KJV)

And it shall come to pass afterward, that I will pour out my _____ upon all flesh; and your sons and your daughters shall _____, your old men shall dream dreams, your young men shall see visions: And also upon the servants and upon the handmaids in those days will I pour out my _____.

EZEKIEL 36:26-27 (KJV)

A new heart also will I give you, and a new _____ will I put within you: and I will take away the _____ heart out of your flesh, and I will give you an heart of _____. And I will put My _____ within you and cause you to walk in my statues, and ye shall keep my judgments, and do them.

ISAIAH 28:10-12 (KJV)

For precept must be upon precept, precept upon precept; line upon line, line upon line; here a little, and there a little: For with stammering lips and another _____will he _____ to this people. To whom he said, This is the _____ wherewith ye may cause the weary to rest; and this is the _____: yet they would not hear.

JEREMIAH 31:33 (KJV)

But this shall be the _____ that I will make with the house of Israel; After those days, saith the LORD, I will put my _____ in their inward parts, and _____ it in their hearts; and will be their God, and they shall be my people.

What prophecy did Joel make regarding God's Spirit?

How would the outpouring of God's Spirit impact the heart?

What two benefits of the Holy Spirit were prophesied in Isaiah 28:12?

Several prophets in the Old Testament prophesied the outpouring of God's Spirit. It was clearly stated that the Spirit would be given to male and female, as well as bond or free; there would be no respecter of persons. Ezekiel's prophecy explained that God's Spirit would change the heart of the believer; recall the scriptures that describe the *circumcision of the heart* (reference: Colossians 2:11). With the infilling of the Holy Spirit, the believer would also receive *rest* and *refreshing*.

NEW TESTAMENT PROPHECY
Read John 3:1-8
What two births did Jesus tell Nicodemus were required to enter the kingdom of God?

What does it mean to be "born of the Spirit?"

Is being born of the Spirit essential for salvation?

_____

_____

_____

During Jesus' discussion with Nicodemus, He clearly states that a person must be _born again_ to see/enter the kingdom of God. Although Nicodemus struggled to understand this concept, Jesus was speaking of that which would come on the Day of Pentecost as recorded in Acts 2. As Jesus stated, being born again of the Spirit is essential for entry into the kingdom of God (salvation).

Fill in the blanks:

MARK 16:17-18 (KJV)

And these signs shall follow them that believe; In my name shall they cast out devils; they shall _____ with new _____; They shall take up serpents; and if they drink any deadly thing, it shall not hurt them; they shall lay hands on the sick, and they shall

_____.

What are the four characteristics that will follow believers?

_____

_____

_____

Did you notice the similarity between Isaiah's prophecy (Old Testament) and the verses in the 16th chapter of Mark (New Testament)? Both passages of scripture mention speaking in a new tongue, another language. As we continue with our study, we should look to learn when and where these prophecies were fulfilled.

Read Acts 1:8

What did Jesus tell his disciples they would receive after the Holy Ghost came on them?

THE LONG-AWAITED DAY ARRIVES: THE OUTPOURING OF THE HOLY SPIRIT

Read Acts 2:1-8

Complete the table below by writing the keywords and phrases from each of the verses.

Verse	Key Words / Phrases
1	
2	
3	
4	
5	
6	
7	
8	

In obedience to Jesus, the disciples returned to Jerusalem and waited for the "power from on high" that Jesus promised. Then, 50 days after Christ rested in the tomb (the anniversary date of the Israelites walking out of Egypt as free men and women), an amazing event took place (reference the study on the Feast of Pentecost).

The sound of a mighty wind filled the room, and fire came down and sat upon each one, showing the divine presence of God. They all experienced the infilling of the Holy Ghost (Spirit) and began to speak in other tongues as the Spirit spoke through them.

Even though those receiving the Holy Spirit did not understand the language they were speaking, the Jews from other nations who had gathered at Jerusalem for the Feast of Pentecost understood the language being spoken by the local Galileans.

At this moment, the Dispensation of the Law ended and the Dispensation of Grace began (see Appendix C). For the first time in history, believers who obeyed the Gospel experienced spiritual rebirth. It was just as Jesus had described to Nicodemus in John, chapter 3. In fulfillment of the Old Testament prophecies, God's gift of a new covenant became available to all who believe and obey His Gospel.

THE HOLY SPIRIT IS RESURRECTION POWER
Read Romans 8:9-11

What is God's promise to those who have been filled with the Holy Spirit?

Is it possible for a person to belong to Christ and not have the Holy Spirit?

Read 1 Corinthians 15:52-54
Read 1 Thessalonians 4:16-17
Read Ephesians 2:5

According to these scriptures, what will happen to those who are filled with the Holy Spirit when Christ comes for His Church?

What did Paul mean by the statement "the mortal shall put on immortality?"

From these verses, we learn that those who are filled with the Holy Spirit will be changed in the twinkling of an eye, putting on immortality. The Holy Spirit is the resurrection power of God, which will quicken the mortal bodies of those having His Spirit. Then, when the trumpet of God sounds, they will be caught up to meet Him in the air to be with Him for all eternity. It is the hope of eternal life for those who are in Christ Jesus.

EXAMPLE OF BELIEVERS RECEIVING THE HOLY SPIRIT

Read Acts 19:1-6

Why did Paul command the believers at Ephesus to be baptized again?

Did they receive the gift of the Holy Spirit at the time they were baptized in the name of Jesus, or later?

What was the evidence that the believers had received the Holy Spirit?

_____

_____

In this example, we can safely assume that the believers at Ephesus had fully repented of their sins since they were followers of John the Baptist. At the beginning of this account, the believers had only been baptized under John's baptism.

Paul reminded them that John merely baptized unto repentance, but John advised the people that they should believe on Him who would come after him. Notice that the believers were then baptized a second time in the name of the Lord Jesus. However, they did not automatically receive the gift of the Holy Spirit the moment they rose from the water baptism.

As Paul laid hands on them, they received the Holy Spirit. In this example, we learn that baptism and receiving the Holy Spirit are two independent events.

There are other similar examples which confirm that baptism and receiving the Holy Spirit are independent events (reference Acts 8:12-16 and Acts 10:44-48 for additional examples).

Water baptism and the infilling of the Holy Spirit are separate events.

CONCLUSION:

Receiving the Holy Spirit is the last step in the pattern of redemption for believers today. As a reminder of the conclusion from the study on "Obeying the Gospel of Jesus Christ", please review the correlation below between the Gospel and steps for obeying the Gospel shown on the illustrations at the top of the next page:

Christ died **Crucified**	Christ was **Buried**	Christ **Resurrected**
Believer dies **Repentance**	Believer buried **Baptism**	Believer resurrects **Holy Spirit**

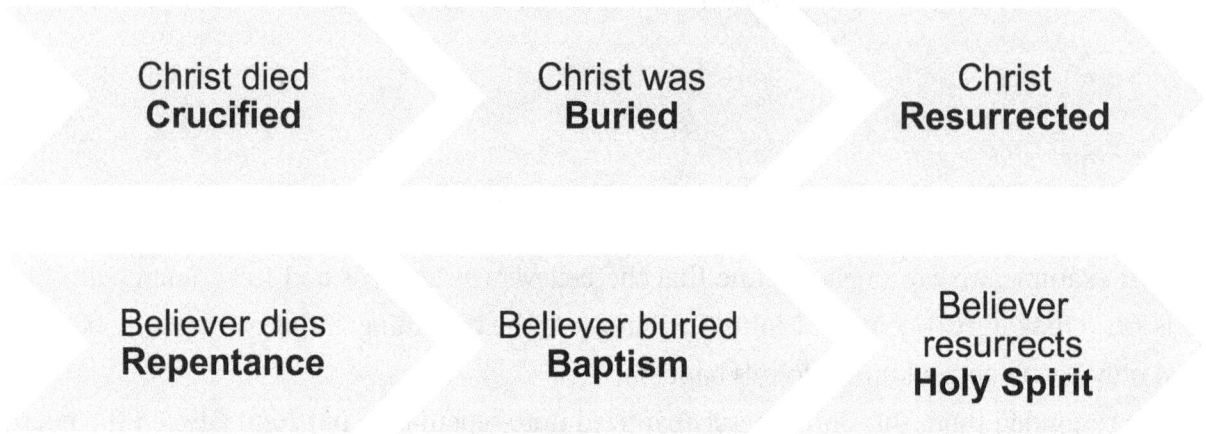

Whenever a believer does their part (repentance and baptism), God offers them the gift of the Holy Spirit. Once a believer accepts the gift from God, they experience the infilling of the Holy Spirit.

There is one example in Acts 10:44-48, where Cornelius and his household received the Holy Spirit during Peter's sermon (before they were baptized). How is it possible for a person to be born again of the spirit before being buried (baptism)? Do you recall our study on atonement? Whenever a person repents (typology of death), their sins are forgiven; the blood of Jesus is applied to their sins and atones for their sins.

Therefore, their sins are covered, and essentially God chooses to overlook them. Thus, they can technically receive the Holy Spirit before burying their sins in baptism. As in the case with Cornelius, Peter insisted that they be baptized in the name of Jesus, to remit/remove their sins (reference Acts 2:38).

We established in this study that the infilling of the Holy Spirit is essential for salvation. The parable of the 10 virgins (reference Matthew 25:1-14) is a clear warning that one must have and maintain the Holy Spirit to be saved whenever Christ comes to collect His bride (the Church). From our study of the Tabernacle, we learned that the oil in the Menorah represented the Holy Spirit. Likewise, the oil in the lamps of the 10 virgins is a typology of the Holy Spirit.

What happens to a believer when they receive the infilling of the Holy Spirit? Recall that we established in prior studies that our spirits are dead because of sin, and all have inherited sin. As Jesus explained to Nicodemus in John chapter 3, whenever we receive the Holy Spirit, our spirit experiences new birth and becomes alive (resurrected) within us. Although the death of our sinful, carnal nature may be a lengthy process, the new birth of our spirit with the infilling of the Holy Spirit is instantaneous.

If you have not experienced the infilling of the Holy Spirit, I hope and pray that you will seek God for this incredible gift. In my experience, receiving the Holy Spirit is the most thrilling encounter with God that a person can experience on this side of eternity. In 1 Peter 1:8, Peter refers to the Holy Spirit as joy unspeakable and full of glory. Philippians 4:7 describes it as the peace that passes all understanding.

But the best benefit of all is the hope of eternal life with our Lord and Savior Jesus Christ. The gift of the Holy Spirit is free to all who obey His Gospel, regardless of their status in life (reference Titus 2:11-14). Paul made it clear in his letter to the Church in Ephesus (reference Ephesians 2:8-9) that the Holy Spirit cannot be purchased or earned through good works, so that no one could boast. It is only through His grace and kindness toward mankind that He purchased our redemption by His sacrifice at Calvary.

Even the angels in heaven desire to understand God's mercy towards mankind (1 Peter 1:12). When one third of the angels rebelled against God, they were expelled from heaven like a lightning bolt, with no means of redemption (reference Luke 10:18). Yet, when mankind disobeyed God, we received mercy and the means for redemption.

The Holy Spirit is Resurrection Power!

SELF-REFLECTIONS:

What new Biblical revelations did you gain from this study?

How does it make you feel to realize that the angels desire to understand God's sacrifice for the redemption available to you?

If you have received the Holy Spirit, how are you ensuring the *oil in your lamp* (the Holy Spirit) does not run dry?

GUIDELINES FOR BIBLE STUDY LEADERS

INTRODUCTION:

In 2024, someone asked me to show them how to be a Bible study leader. After giving the request some thought, I agreed to meet with them and impart some of my experience. Through writing this book, I understood that sharing my experience might help those aspiring to become Bible study leaders. There may also be those already leading Bible Studies, but may not have the experience to feel confident in the role of Bible Study Leader. I hope this section of the book will provide you with some ideas to incorporate into your current strategy.

Depending on your personality style, it may be easier to gain that experience by leading your family or close friends in a Bible Study. Once you've led a few studies, you'll see leadership isn't as tough as you think.

Whenever you lead Bible Studies with those outside of your family and close friends, invite an experienced Bible study leader to accompany you. Ask them to provide you with feedback, privately, after the event is completed. Knowing that a knowledgeable person is there to jump in and assist with any difficult situations or questions should give you additional confidence.

FRIENDSHIP EVANGELISM:

Aaron, who is a close friend of mine, has a magnetic, open personality. He is so dynamic that people have approached him in public on numerous occasions and started a conversation. Using his spiritual wisdom, he can quickly turn a discussion with a stranger towards God and His redeeming power. Typically, my friend will partner with me if a new acquaintance is open to learning more about God's plan for salvation. I always smile whenever Aaron calls to say, "A guy approached me at the store. He is hungry for God. When can you give him a Bible Study?"

If you have a personality similar to my friend's, then you should have no problem finding someone to share God's word with. However, if you are more like me and less approachable, allow me to share my approach, which I describe as *friendship evangelism*. The first step is to become a friend. If it is a neighbor, co-worker, or family member, get to know them. The closer a friend *you* become, the more the person will open up to you about their life and life issues.

Once they have confided in you, then carefully minister to them by praying for their needs and sharing your personal testimony about how God has changed your life. Work to build their trust and live a Godly example in their presence so they will recognize something special about your life. If they are not open to learning about God and His word, do not push them.

Remember that they have free will. Pushing will only repel them and may damage the relationship. However, if they are open to learning more, then you have a chance to share the Gospel with them.

Many Christians are not comfortable sharing God's word with someone. Instead, they attempt to entice the person to attend their church. In my experience, people feel more at ease discussing salvation with a friend in a casual setting, rather than a church service. If you are not practicing friendship evangelism, I suggest you consider giving this approach a try.

PLANNING AND PREPARATIONS:

Before conducting a Bible Study, you must follow three important steps:

1. Prepare,
2. Prepare, and
3. Prepare!

If this is the first session with a new person or group, it is important to understand their Bible knowledge and spiritual maturity. Have they obeyed the Gospel of Jesus Christ for salvation? Do they have a basic understanding of the Bible? I have worked with those who did not know there was an Old Testament and a New Testament. In one case, the person had never owned a Bible.

On the other hand, I have worked with people who had a deep knowledge of the Bible but had been poisoned by religion and were seeking a genuine relationship with God. Knowing their Bible knowledge and spiritual standing with God will be beneficial as you plan your Bible Study.

Prepare the Bible Study material you wish to present. If your audience has not experienced salvation, begin with the simple Gospel message and how to obey the Gospel for salvation. I personally feel compelled to share the Gospel with all who will listen.

After deciding on the specific Bible study to present, think about the materials you'll need. Gather the materials needed in advance and ensure you have *read and understand* all the material to be used. For example, if you're not familiar with where certain books are located within the Bible or how to find information quickly in a concordance, then work this out before you get in front of others. Familiarize yourself with the material in advance to avoid delays in the time allotted for your Bible study.

Make sure all printouts and other materials are ready for the first session. Have pens or pencils readily available for participants. A coffee cup full of pens and highlighters sits on the table when I conduct studies.

At the introduction of this book, I provided information regarding the various Bible translations. It's best only to use one Bible translation for the studies. It can become confusing when people use different translations while reading.

Create an agenda and ensure it leaves plenty of time for questions and discussions. Typically, allocate around twenty minutes for discussion in a one-hour Bible Study. If snacks and drinks are on the menu, give the audience time to serve themselves before starting.

CONDUCTING THE BIBLE STUDY:

Below is a simple agenda that you may find beneficial.

- Greeting/Introduction
  - o Welcome everyone, and offer a brief introduction to the lesson.
- Prayer Requests
  - o Inquire about prayer needs (write them down).
- Opening Prayer
  - o Pray for the study itself and for any requests that have been made.
- Bible Study
  - o Pass out materials for the session. (If you hand them out at the beginning, participants may become distracted.)
  - o Conduct the Bible Study.
- Final Remarks
  - o Provide information about the next study.
  - o Include directives about the assignments to be completed before the next gathering.
  - o Review the key points discussed from the study, then encourage practical application.
  - o Thank participants for coming; ensure everyone feels welcome to return.
- Closing Prayer

FURTHER CONSIDERATIONS FOR SUCCESS:

Listed below are some additional suggestions that will aid in leading a group Bible study.

- **Follow an agenda:**
  - Leave plenty of time for discussions and questions.
  - Be respectful of their time and keep it brief (1 hour).
  - Stay focused.

- **Keep your guests in mind:**
  - Ensure participants are comfortable.
  - Be sensitive to their responses and participation and adjust if needed.
  - Avoid embarrassing any of the participants.
  - Meet guests where they are spiritually, not where you wish they would be. Never make light of their spiritual experiences.
  - Rather than telling someone they are "wrong" about an answer, redirect their thoughts to another perspective, such as:
    - "What else might this mean?"
    - "In my view, this means ... "
    - "I see this verse differently; consider this meaning ... "
    - "I have learned that this verse is saying ... "
    - "Theologians believe ... "

- **Encourage participation:**
  - Ask What-, Why-, How-, When-, and Who- questions that are open-ended and can't be quickly answered with a "yes" or "no".
  - Take turns reading the scriptures (if they are comfortable reading).
  - A Bible study isn't the time/place to argue about religious beliefs or differences in opinions. Steer clear of discussions on religious doctrine. *(cont'd next page)*

- **Remain spiritually focused:**
  - Stay in the Word.
  - If / when they appear ready, offer and arrange for their baptism.
  - Offer additional Bible studies if they are open to learning more.
  - If you don't know the answer to a question, reassure them you will provide one—even if it requires a follow-up after the study. Don't guess; acknowledge you don't know, and we'll find the best answer as a group.
  - Keep the conversation centered on the topics at hand. Redirect and re-focus when necessary.
  - Refrain from becoming their enemy if they don't accept the Gospel; remain their friend. Paul spoke about those who *plant* and others who *water.* You are still an instrument in their spiritual growth.
  - Encourage one another and build each other up in the Lord; the Bible commands this in 1 Thessalonians 5:11!

BRIEF STUDIES TO USE

The following are four short Bible studies for use when you have limited time. My Bible students have shown great interest in these tried and tested topics, each with its own spiritual meaning. May these Bible studies be a blessing for you, as well.

#1: *The Name of God*

INTRODUCTION:

As humans, we tend to place much emphasis on names. I have witnessed expecting parents who invested many hours of research and discussion to arrive at the perfect name for their new baby. Across the generations of time, men sought to know the name of God. While there were many descriptions of God revealed to mankind throughout the Bible, the name of the Messiah was finally revealed to Mary as recorded in Luke 1:31. The QR code featured for this study takes leaders to an interesting article about *"Breathing the Name YAHWEH,"* which will provide an additional context for this study.

MOSES INQUIRES OF GOD'S NAME:

Exodus 3:13-14 (KJV): God tells Moses that He is "I am that I am." According to Jewish historians, Moses heard an *inhalation* and *exhalation*. Moses interpreted this breath phonetically as "YH-WY". Perhaps God was saying: "I AM the BREATH of LIFE."

- In Hebrew, the name of God was "YAHWEH."
- In Greek, the translation of YAHWEH is "JEHOVAH."

THE ANGEL REVEALS THE MESSIAH'S NAME:

Luke 1:31 states, "You shall call His name Jesus." The angel prophesied to Mary that she would conceive a son by the Holy Spirit and call His name Jesus.

Matthew 1:21 teaches that "You shall call His name Jesus, for He shall save His people from their sins." The angel prophesied to Joseph that Mary would conceive a son by the Holy Spirit. The angel gave Joseph the same name for the Messiah that he had given to Mary.

- The interpretation of the name Jesus/Yeshua:
  - The name "Jesus" translated (in Greek) means: "Jehovah is Salvation".
  - In Hebrew, the name "Jesus" is "Yeshua," which means "Yahweh is Salvation".

OLD TESTAMENT DESCRIPTIONS OF GOD:

- Adonai - Lord/Master
- El Shaddai - Lord God Almighty
- El Elyon - The Most High God
- El Olam - The Everlasting God
- Elohim - God
- Jehovah Rohi - Shepherd (The Lord is my shepherd)
- Jehovah Jireh - Provider (I shall not want)
- Jehovah Shalom - Peace (He makes me to lie down in green pastures)
- Jehovah Rapha - Healer (He restoreth my soul)
- Jehovah Tsidkenu - Righteousness (He leads me on paths of righteousness)
- Jehovah Shammah - Who is there (Yea, though I walk through the valley of death, thou art with me)
- Jehovah Nissi - Banner (Thou preparest a table before me in the presence of my enemies)
- Jehovah M'Kaddesh- Sanctifies (Thou anointest my head with oil)

#2: *The Garden of Gethsemane*

INTRODUCTION:

The place called *Gethsemane* is mentioned explicitly only twice in the Bible. Yet, the Garden of Gethsemane is monumental in that Jesus chose this location to pray after His last supper with the disciples. It was here that Jesus was arrested and would later be crucified. A closer look at Gethsemane and the Kidron Brook, which ran through the valley of Gethsemane, reveals typologies of Christ and His sacrifice.

LOCATION:

Gethsemane was located just east of the Temple Mount, with the Kidron Brook running in the valley between Gethsemane and the Temple.

The Kidron (Hebrew)/Cedron (Greek) Brook was used to drain sacrificial blood from the Temple. The years of blood flow left the brook stained. The QR code shown above takes you to an expanded version of the map, which features Jerusalem at the time of Jesus.

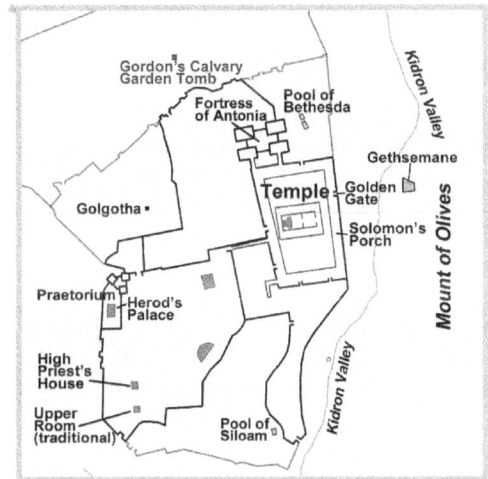

JESUS CROSSED KIDRON / CEDRON BROOK:

After the Lord's final supper with his disciples, Jesus departed the upper room and made His way to Gethsemane. In John 18:1, it is recorded that Jesus and His disciples crossed over the brook Cedron. Imagine the emotions that Jesus must have experienced as He stepped over the brook, which was stained from the flow of blood after years of animal sacrifices. The blood-stained brook must have been a stark reminder that the blood that encompassed His body would be shed before the day was finished.

GETHSEMANE:

Gethsemane means "oil press". Historians believe there was an olive press at the base of the Garden of Gethsemane, thus giving the place its name. On the hill, east of the olive press, was an olive grove. Gethsemane was where the olives were *crushed* to yield the oil that was used for the ceremonial anointing of Kings and the burning of oil in lamps. Recall that oil burned in the Menorah inside the Holy of Holies provided the only light.

Consider how Jesus was *crushed* under the weight of the pending suffering that He was soon to endure. Mark 14:32-36 describes the sorrow and agony that Christ experienced. Luke 22:44 records that from Jesus came great drops of blood as He pleaded for God to rescue Him from His pending death. We have already established that olive oil is symbolic of the Holy Spirit. Just as crushing the olives yielded olive oil, the crushing of Jesus and His death yielded the Holy Spirit.

CONTRAST OF TWO GARDENS:

If we contrast the Garden of Eden and the Garden of Gethsemane, we gain additional insight into God's redemption. In the Garden of Eden, the first man, Adam, lived in paradise, but chose to disobey and sin against God. Thus, he was driven from the Garden of Eden and lost access to paradise and his spiritual relationship to God.

However, in the Garden of Gethsemane, Jesus is described as the second Adam in 1 Corinthians 15:45. Although the Garden of Gethsemane was not a paradise, the second Adam, Jesus, chose obedience to God. He suffered the penalty for sin that Adam brought upon all of mankind.

Mankind could never return to God's Garden. We needed a mediator between mankind and God. Jesus became the one mediator to make a way for restoration and reconciliation to God.

For there is one God, and one mediator between God and men, the man Christ Jesus;
1 Timothy 2:5 (KJV)

#3: The Galilean Wedding

INTRODUCTION:

Jesus often used parables and references to natural/cultural events to provide insight into the kingdom of God. Throughout the New Testament, the Church is often referred to as the "bride of Christ" (reference Matthew 9:15 and John 3:29). The Jews of that era were familiar with the rituals of a Galilean Wedding.

Jesus utilized this knowledge to teach them about the relationship between Christ and the Church of believers. Below are the ways a Galilean wedding contrasts with Jesus Christ's return to gather His Church (His Bride). The QR code above takes you to a website that foreshadows the biblical rapture to the Marriage Feast of the Lamb.

ENGAGEMENT:

Some typical expectations for a Galilean wedding are listed below.

- The father selects (calls) the bride.
- The man offers a covenant/proposal to the woman.
- Gifts are then exchanged.
- The man offers the woman a *Cup of Joy* (wine).
- The woman has *free will* to accept or reject the Cup of Joy.
- If the woman drinks from the cup, the man then seals the engagement.
- The groom states, "You are now consecrated to me by the laws of Moses, and I will not drink from this cup again until I drink it with you in my father's house."
- The groom leaves until the day the wedding is consummated.
- Only the groom's father knows the day and time that the wedding will take place.
- The father waits until all preparations are complete (approximately one year).

THE LAST SUPPER (MATTHEW 26:29):

God chooses His bride. 1 Corinthians teaches that we were "called by God."

God is faithful, who has called you into fellowship with his Son,
Jesus Christ our Lord.
1 Corinthians 1:9 (NIV)

Jesus offers his disciples a cup of wine, which symbolizes the New Covenant. In the book of Matthew, after the disciples drink from the cup, Jesus states words similar to the Galilean Wedding:

"I tell you, I will not drink from this fruit of the vine from now on
until that day that I drink it new with you in my Father's kingdom."
Matthew 26:29 (NIV)

During communion services, we are reminded of this covenant. No one knows the day and time of the rapture of the Church; only God knows (see Matthew 24:36-38).

But of that day and hour knoweth no man,
no, not the angels of heaven, but my Father only.
Matthew 24:36 (KJV)

PREPARING A NEW PLACE:

-GALILEAN WEDDING

After the engagement, the groom would go away to his father's house to prepare a place for his bride. Typically, this would be adding a room to the father's house. The room would be furnished with furniture, tables, stools, etc. The groom would then prepare for the wedding feast with lamps, oil, rugs, etc.

-JESUS ASCENDS TO HEAVEN TO PREPARE A PLACE

John 14:3 (KJV) states, "And if I go and prepare a place for you, I will come again, and receive you unto myself; that where I am, there ye may be also." This text introduces the doctrine of the Rapture.

BRIDE PREPARATIONS:

-GALILEAN WEDDING

The bride and bridesmaids would select wedding clothing to prepare for the wedding. Fine linen and fabric were not readily available in this era. It could take months to obtain the material for the wedding clothing. Once the clothes were ready (and the first anniversary of the engagement drew near), the bride and bridesmaids would dress and wait in their wedding attire.

They waited to be alerted by the shofar, which would announce the groom's return, and would even sleep in their clothes because the groom typically came in the night. The bride and bridesmaids would need to have lanterns with oil ready to light their path.

CHURCH'S PREPARATIONS:

Matthew 25:1-13 teaches the Parable of the Ten Bridesmaids. Five wise bridesmaids had oil in their lamps. And five foolish bridesmaids had no oil in their lamps. Oil is a type and shadow of the Holy Spirit. The Church must stay full of the Holy Spirit.

> *But if the Spirit of him that raised up Jesus from the dead dwells in you,*
> *he that raised up Christ from the dead shall also quicken your mortal bodies*
> *by his Spirit that dwelleth in you.*
> *Romans 8:11 (KJV)*

DAY OF WEDDING:

-GALILEAN WEDDING

Finally, the father looks and declares all is ready. He tells his son, "Go get your bride." The groom and company walk through the town sounding the shofar to alert the bride. The bride and

196 – GREGORY C. OLIVER

bridesmaids have their lamps full of oil and lit and go to meet the groom. When the groom sees his bride, she is lifted onto a chair and carried to the father's house. Once they enter the father's house, the door is shut, and no one can enter or leave until the wedding feast is completed.

RAPTURE OF THE CHURCH / MARRIAGE SUPPER OF THE LAMB:

- The Church is advised to stay ready. (1 Thessalonians 5:1-6 [KJV])
- The Lord so cometh as a thief in the night. (1 Thessalonians 5:2b)
- We must watch and be sober. (1 Thessalonians 5:6b)
- Reference parable of the Ten Bridesmaids, (Matthew 25:1-13 [KJV])

Watch therefore, for ye know neither the day nor the hour
wherein the Son of man cometh. Matthew 25:13 (KJV)

- Jesus will return for his Bride. (1 Thessalonians 4:16-17 [KJV])

For the Lord himself shall descend from heaven with a shout
. . . and with the trump of God: and the dead in Christ will rise first.
Then we which are alive and remain shall be caught up
together with them in the clouds.
1 Thessalonians 4:16, 17a

The Church will be lifted into the air, just as the Galilean bride was lifted into the air.

- Jesus and his bride (the Church) will be joined at the Marriage Supper of the Lamb. (Revelations 19:6-9 [KJV])
- The marriage of the Lamb is come, and his wife has made herself ready. (Revelation 19:7b)
- Blessed are they who are called unto the marriage supper of the Lamb. (Revelation 19:9a)

#4: East

INTRODUCTION:

A careful study of the directions referenced in the Bible reveals the direction *East* to have significance. The following scriptures and proof highlight the East's significance. The scripture list is only an example and isn't meant to be comprehensive. There may be many more examples not included herein.

OLD TESTAMENT:

- Genesis 3:24: God drove Adam and Eve out of the *east* gate of the Garden
- Genesis 4:16: Cain went away from the Lord; to the *east*
- Genesis 13:11: Lot separated from Abraham and journeyed *east*
- Genesis 25:6: Abraham sent the sons of his concubines away to the *east*
- Genesis 41:6: Pharaoh's dream; the *east* wind dried up seven ears of corn (KJV). NOTE: The NIV says, "heads of grain."
- Exodus 10:13: The *east* wind brought in a plague of locusts
- Exodus 14:21: Parting of the Red Sea by the *east* wind
- Exodus 27:13: The Gate to the Tabernacle was on the *east* side

NEW TESTAMENT:

- Matthew 2:1-2, 9: Wise men from the *east* saw a star in the *east* and came to worship Jesus
- Matthew 24:27: Christ's second coming will be from the *eastern* sky
- Jesus' triumphal entry was through the *eastern* gate of Jerusalem (as mentioned in John 12). Refer to the map on the following page for further clarity.

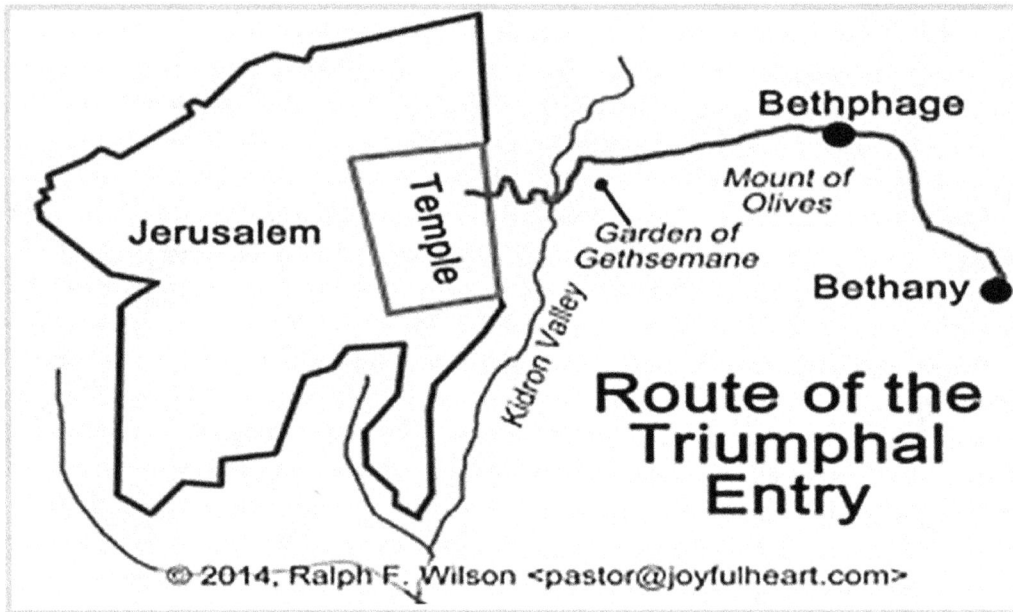

Route of the Triumphal Entry

© 2014, Ralph F. Wilson <pastor@joyfulheart.com>

Moving from *east* to west corresponds with God's direction or moving towards God. Moving from the west towards the east appears to be the opposite of God's direction. For example, Adam and Eve were driven out of the **east** gate of the Garden of Eden (see Genesis 3:24). Therefore, they were driven in an **eastward** direction, which would have been away from paradise and the presence of God.

SUMMARY

During Jesus' ministry, He often resorted to parables to relate to His audience. By referring to natural phenomena, He was able to use numerous analogies to reveal spiritual truths to those who were open to hearing about the coming of the kingdom of God.

In John 12:23-26, we read where Jesus described a seed of grain dying, being planted, and then bringing forth new life, producing much fruit. In this passage, he made the analogy that just as the seed had to die and be buried, so would the Messiah have to die and be buried. Just as the buried seed brings forth new life, so would the Messiah be resurrected to new life.

Scientists cannot fully explain how a dead and buried seed can sprout into new life. Yet, the process of taking a seed and planting it to experience new life is simplistic enough for even a child to understand. I recall my wife teaching first graders about plant life cycles. As part of her lessons, she would lead the students in an experiment where each student buried a seed (bean) in a clear, plastic container. Each day, the students would observe in amazement as the seed began to sprout and push its stem toward the surface. Within a few weeks, each student was the proud owner of a new living plant.

Could the pattern of redemption really be as simple as the analogy of the seed? Yes! As I have established with these studies, the simple pattern of redemption is repeated throughout the Bible. For those who seek to have an intimate relationship with God and are willing to study His Word, the pattern of redemption becomes visible.

Perhaps the reason God orchestrated various events throughout history to reflect the pattern of redemption is so that God could point the way to those who are truly hungry for salvation. Maybe it was God's way of saying, "Look, here it is; here is the pattern of redemption. Do not miss it!"

Matthew 13:18-23 records another parable of the seed, which is sown on different types of soil. Only the seed that fell on good ground survived to bring forth new life. In this analogy, the seed was the Word of God; the ground was the human heart. In closing, I pray that each person who encounters these Bible Studies will condition their heart to be good ground.

The Pattern of Redemption:

- Death/Repentance

- Burial/Baptism

- Resurrection

APPENDIX

A. HEBREW CALENDAR

B. SEVEN CONVOCATIONS OF THE OLD TESTAMENT

C. DISPENSATIONS OF TIME

D. BIBLICAL COVENANTS

E. HEBREW 24-HOUR DAY

F. TRIBES OF ISRAEL

G. TEN EGYPTIAN PLAGUES AGAINST EGYPTIAN GODS

H. PATTERN OF THE GOSPEL OF JESUS CHRIST

APPENDIX A:

HEBREW CALENDAR

Leviticus 23

	Month	No of Days	Holy Convocations
APR	Nisan	30	14 Lord's Passover 15 Feast of Passover 15 – 21 Feast of Unleavened Bread 16 Feast of First-fruits
MAY	Iyyar	29	
JUN	Sivan	30	6 Feast of Pentecost - Feast of Weeks
JUL	Tammuz	29	
AUG	Ab	30	
SEP	Elul	29	
OCT	Tishri	30	1 Feast of Trumpet 10 Day of Atonement 15 Feast of Tabernacle - Booths
NOV	Heshvan	29/30	
DEC	Chislev	30/29	
JAN	Tebeth	29	
FEB	Shebat	30	
MAR	Adar	29	
	Veadar Intercalary month 7 times / 19 years	30/29	

APPENDIX B:

SEVEN CONVOCATIONS OF THE OLD TESTAMENT

LEVITICUS 23RD CHAPTER:

1. Passover – Nisan 14 (Lord's Passover) 15 Passover of Death Angel
   Pesach (Hebrew)
2. Unleavened Bread – Nisan 15-21
   Matzah (Hebrew)
3. First Fruit – Nisan 16
   Hag HaBikkurim (Hebrew)
4. Pentecost (Feast of Weeks) – Sivan 6
   Shavuot (Hebrew)
5. Trumpets – Tishri 1
   Yom Teruah (Hebrew)
6. Day of Atonement – Tishri 10th
   Yom Kippur (Hebrew)
7. Tabernacles (Booths) – Tishri 15
   Sukkot (Hebrew)

KEY POINTS:

- The seven convocations (six feasts and one fast) of the Old Testament had spiritual symbolism.
- Seven is God's number for completeness; thus, seven convocations.
- Other Jewish holidays do not involve feasts (not listed here).
- Jewish history provides insight into these events that is not always included in the Biblical account.
- Most of these convocations commemorated specific events in Jewish history.
- Some aspects of the feasts are types and shadows of prophecies yet to be fulfilled.

APPENDIX C:

DISPENSATIONS OF TIME

1 - INNOCENCE

- Began with Creation (Genesis 1:26-31)
- Adam and Eve in the Garden
- Ended with the fall of man (partaking of the fruit of the knowledge of good and evil)

2 - CONSCIENCE

- Began with the fall of man (Genesis 3:6-24)
- Cain killed Abel
- Mankind grew evil
- Ended with the great flood/Noah

3 - HUMAN GOVERNANCE

- Began with the great flood (Genesis 7:16-24)
- Nimrod—building of the Tower of Babel
- Mankind grew evil
- Ended with God's covenant with Abraham

4 - PROMISE

- Began with God's covenant with Abraham (Genesis 17:2-14)
- Abraham/Isaac/Jacob/Egyptian slavery/Moses
- Ended at Mount Sinai with the giving of the law

5 - LAW

- Began with the giving of the law at Mount Sinai (Exodus 19:18- 20:18)
- Journey to Promise Land
- History of the twelve tribes of Israel
- Life and ministry of Jesus
- Ended with an outpouring of the Holy Ghost on the day of Pentecost

6 - GRACE

- Began with an outpouring of the Holy Ghost on the day of Pentecost (Acts 2:1-8)
- History of the early New Testament Church
- Will end with the Battle of Armageddon (Revelation, Chapters 16 & 17)

7 - KINGDOM REIGN

- 1000-year reign of Christ
- Great White Throne Judgment
- Eternity

APPENDIX D:

BIBLICAL COVENANTS

	Covenant	Reference	Condition	Specifics
1	Adamic[1]	Genesis 2:15-17	Conditional	Placed in the Garden of Eden. Forbidden to eat of the Tree of the Knowledge of Good and Evil.
2	Noahic[2]	Genesis 6:18 Genesis 9:9-17	Unconditional	A flood will never again destroy the world.
3	Abrahamic[3]	Genesis 17:1-27 Genesis 22:15-18	Conditional	Abraham's seed would inherit the Promised Land. Abraham's seed numbered like sand and stars. They will be God's chosen people.
4	Sinaitic[4]	Exodus 19:5 Exodus 20:1-18	Conditional	Giving of the Ten Commandments and the Law.
5	Phinehas	Numbers 25:1-13	Unconditional	Peace: Phinehas' seed would be priests forever (see genealogy of Mary).
6	Davidic	2 Samuel 7:15-16	Unconditional	David's dynasty/kingdom would rule forever (see Jesus' reign).
7	New[5]	Jeremiah 31:31-32	Conditional	Obey the Gospel for everlasting life.

[1] Beginning of Dispensation of Innocence

[2] Beginning of Dispensation of Human Governance

[3] Beginning of Dispensation of Promise

[4] Beginning of Dispensation of The Law

[5] Beginning of Dispensation of Grace

APPENDIX E:

HEBREW 24-HOUR DAY

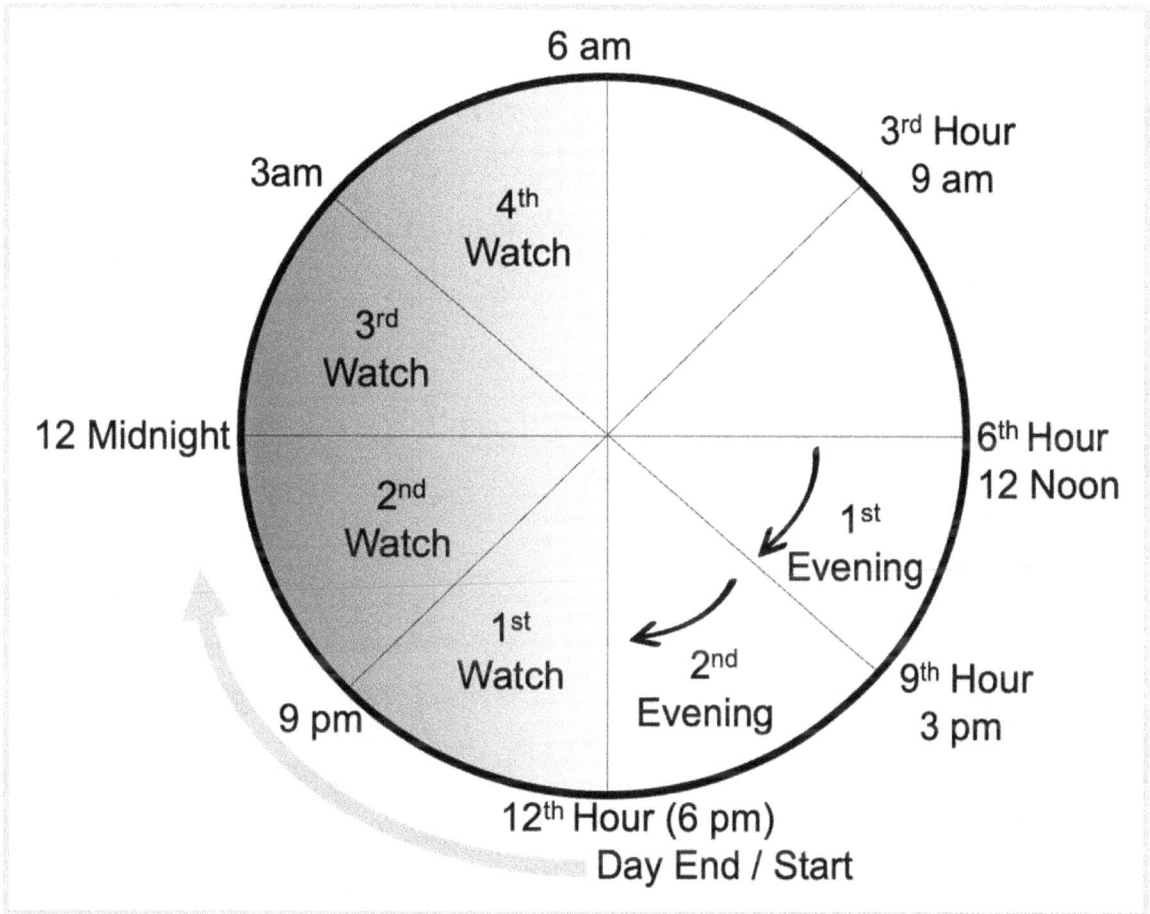

A sundial was used during daylight hours.

Reference found in the QR code:

APPENDIX F:

TRIBES OF ISRAEL

12 Patriarchs Jacob's Sons		MOTHERS			
		Leah	Bihah Rachael's Handmaid	Zilpah Leah's Handmaid	Rachael
1	Reuben	✓			
2	Simeon	✓			
3	Levi	✓			
4	Judah	✓			
5	Dan		✓		
6	Naphtali		✓		
7	Gad			✓	
8	Asher			✓	
9	Issachar	✓			
10	Zebulun				
11	Joseph				✓
12	Benjamin				✓

Joseph's Sons: **Manasseh and Ephraim**

	Descendants	Granted Land Territory	Comments		12 Tribes in Revelations	Comments
1	Reuben	✓		1	✓	
2	Simeon	✓		2	✓	
	Levi		Granted tithes versus land	3	✓	
3	Judah	✓		4	✓	
4	Dan	✓				Abandoned faith for idol worship; Judges 18
5	Naphtali	✓		5	✓	
6	Gad	✓		6	✓	
7	Asher	✓		7	✓	
8	Issachar	✓		8	✓	
9	Zebulun	✓		9	✓	
	Joseph		Sons granted land on behalf of Joseph	10	✓	
10	Benjamin	✓		11	✓	
11	*Manasseh*	✓		12	✓	
12	*Ephraim*	✓				Abandoned faith for idol worship; Hosea 4:17

APPENDIX G:

TEN EGYPTIAN PLAGUES AGAINST THE EGYPTIAN GODS
(EXODUS, CHAPTERS 7 THROUGH 12)

Below are the ten Egyptian plagues and the corresponding Egyptian gods:

1. God turned the *water into blood*.
    Hapi—the Egyptian god of the Nile
    The water in the Nile was undrinkable for seven days
    All the fish died, and the river stank.

2. God sent swarms of *frogs*.
    Heket (head of a frog): Egyptian goddess of Fertility

3. God sent a plague of *lice*.
    Geb: Egyptian god of the Earth (and dust of the Earth)

4. God sent a plague of *flies*.
    Khepri (head of a fly): Egyptian god of Creation and rebirth

5. God sent a plague that *killed the cattle and livestock*.
    Hathor (head of a cow): Egyptian goddess of love and protection

6. God sent a plague of *dust that caused boils*.
    Isis: Egyptian goddess of medicine and peace

7. God sent a plague *of hail*.
    Nut: Egyptian goddess of the sky
    Most of the remaining livestock and crops were destroyed.

8. God sent *locusts* into the sky, which destroyed the crops.
    Seth: Egyptian god of storms and disorder
    Locusts destroyed all remaining crops

9. God caused *darkness* across Egypt for three days.

   Ra: Egyptian sun god

10. God sent the *Death Angel* across Egypt to slay all firstborn.

    Pharaoh: claimed to be the son of Ra and the god of Egypt

Reference:

APPENDIX H:

THE PATTERN OF THE GOSPEL OF JESUS CHRIST

GOSPEL	DEATH	BURIAL	RESURRECTION
Jesus	**Crucified**	**Buried**	**Rose again 3rd day**
Believer Obeying the Gospel	**Repents** Dying of Carnal Nature	**Baptized** Buried with Christ Jesus	**Receives the Holy Spirit** Spiritual Birth
Noah and His Family	**Repentance** God repented for creating man	**Burial** Flood buried the Earth	**Resurrection** New life without sin after the Flood
Israelite Slaves Redemption from Slavery	**Death of Paschal Lamb** Means to Freedom, Blood saved them from the wrath of God	**Baptism** Baptized in the Red Sea and the cloud	**Received the Law** Resurrected nation with life-changing Law
Tabernacle God's Provision for the atonement of sins	**Death of Sacrifice** Bloodshed at Brazen altar	**Wash in Brazen Laver** Symbolic of baptism which is symbolic of burial	**Sins Atoned** High Priest encounters the presence of God

ACKNOWLEDGEMENTS

I am forever grateful to all those who assisted me in the development of this book.

Foremost, I am grateful to my Lord and Savior, Jesus Christ, who is King and Lord of my life. Without Him, I can do nothing. Everything that I have ever accomplished in life is because of His mercy, grace, and blessings.

I also wish to acknowledge the following people who assisted me with this project:

Retha Oliver, for being my chief editor and my life partner.
Kimerli Oliver, for your excellent wordsmithing.
Hannah and Hunter Oliver, for your input on the book cover.
Charles Johnson, for your help with the Foreword.
Larry Weinert, for your valuable input on the Passover.
Teresa Granberry, for your help in publishing this book.
Sam Granberry, for your inspiration and encouragement.
Sarah Stephens, for your input on this book.
Dr. Brian Bennett, for your inspiration and friendship.
Aaron Matthews, for your friendship and encouragement.
Charles McDaniel, for your friendship and for sharing your knowledge of baptism.
Kristyn Stillwell, for sharing your knowledge of the Garden of Gethsemane.
Ryan Campbell, for sharing your insight into the Galilean Wedding.

ABOUT THE AUTHOR

Gregory C. Oliver and his wife reside in the Texas Hill Country, close to his daughter and son. Greg retired after 42 years of service in the chemical manufacturing business. His three primary interests are Bible research, guitar, and woodworking. He built the cabinetry and woodwork by hand for their home. The Olivers are active in their community and local church.

If you're interested in booking Greg for an event or hope to discuss this Bible study further, you may email him at: gregoliverministry@gmail.com.

www.ingramcontent.com/pod-product-compliance
Lightning Source LLC
Chambersburg PA
CBHW081149270326
41930CB00014B/3087